Intent on Laughter

Intent on Laughter

JOHN BAILEY

Quadrangle / The New York Times Book Co.

Library of Congress Cataloging in Publication Data

Bailey, John
    Intent on laughter.

    Includes index.
    1. Wit and humor—Philosophy. 2. Wit and humor—Psychology.   I. Title.
PN6149.P5B33 1976   827'.009   75-36265
ISBN 0-8129-0621-7

Contents

Acknowledgments

Grateful acknowledgment is made to the proprietors and publishers of the following material for permission to quote:

Dodd, Mead & Company, Inc., for "The Perfect Salesman," from *The Garden of Folly,* by Stephen Leacock.

Houghton Mifflin Company, for "Walloping Window Blind," from *Davy and the Goblin,* by Charles E. Carryl.

Harper & Row, Inc., for "Opera Synopses," by Robert Benchley, from *The Benchley Roundup,* compiled by Nathaniel Benchley.

Simon & Schuster, Inc., for "Eine Kleine Mothmusic," by S. J. Perelman, originally published in *The New Yorker.*

E. P. Dutton & Co., Inc. and William Heinemann Ltd, London, for *Yet Again,* by Max Beerbohm.

The proprietors of *Punch,* London, and the author, for *Punch* columns by Robert Morley.

The Saturday Evening Post for "Note By a Shortsighted Naturalist," "Think of the Earth As a Shrunken Apple," and "I Can't Help My Good Looks." (Reprinted with permission from The Saturday Evening Post.)

McCall's, for "A Chain of Kindness," and "Watch Me Spear This Pumpkin."

Macmillan Publishers Ltd, for *The Trumpet Major,* by Thomas Hardy.

The New Yorker, for "Test" and "The Albatross."

My thanks also to Michael ffolkes, Frank Modell, Whitney Darrow, Jr., Mischa Richter, Charles Saxon, and Ton Smits, for sketches made especially for this book, and to *The New Yorker* and the artists for permission to reprint cartoons by Charles Addams, Whitney Darrow, Jr., Michael ffolkes, Frank Modell, Mischa Richter, Charles Saxon, and Ton Smits.

Preface

Before beginning I will apologize to the reader for the almost complete absence of such phrases as "It seems to me. . . ." Old habits are hard to break and I was born cocksure.

When I was twelve years old an incident occurred which modified this condition. I had selected the straightest branch I could find and made a spear from it. I spent the morning sharpening it and fire-hardening it according to the method outlined in my copy of *Life in the Stone Age*. I then went to the garden and selected the largest pumpkin I could find. I put the pumpkin on the grass near the back door, backed off fifteen feet, and began to cast the spear.

I hit the pumpkin ten times out of twelve. The spear went into the pumpkin with a satisfying *chung* that had me beside myself with pride in my achievement and wonder at my superlative skill and ability. I felt I had to share the moment with someone, and I selected my father. In answer to my repeated cries he appeared at the back door.

"Watch me spear this pumpkin!" I called.

I backed off fifteen feet, cast the spear, and missed. I retrieved the spear, threw it, and missed again. After about thirty misses my father announced that he would have to leave. There was no twitting. Nothing was said about my having missed the pumpkin. He merely disappeared into the house. My own feelings were indescribable. I had been led to believe that I was an invincible spear-thrower. The shock of those thirty misses is still with me today.

In later years, as a youth of eighteen or twenty, it was my custom to announce some great project I was about to undertake and explain that its success was assured because of the unusual power of my intellect, my incredible physical coordination, and my stupefying inborn cleverness.

At the peak of my blathering my father would quietly say, "Watch me spear this pumpkin." He said it as often as he thought it was necessary to deflate me, and in this way I learned humility. But not enough. I will be obliged to the reader if he will insert the phrase "It seems to me . . ." wherever it seems to him to be needed.

Intent on Laughter

1

The Opposite

Humor, according to a definition I have taken some trouble to formulate, because I know they are waiting for me, is a structure which makes a violent attack on the reader's judgment or knowledge, which is successfully defended against by the reader, because the means for a successful defense is built into the structure.

Because the attack must be violent, all humor is based on an opposite. It may take me some time to explain this. Opposites are not necessarily funny. Black and white are opposites, but the opposite is not funny because there has been no attempt to make one think that black is the same thing as white. There must be an attack.

A simple opposite does not necessarily result in peals of laughter for the same reason that the contrast between a high note and a low note struck on the piano does not result in broken sobs. Some further construction is necessary before the emotions will be sufficiently aroused to cause laughter or tears.

Humor must be composed, and its composition requires the same complication as a piece of music.

An opposite is merely the basis of a humor structure, and it can be compared to the armature on which a sculptor fashions a statue. But it is true that sometimes one can more or less see what the statue is going to be, even before the sculptor begins to pat on clay. Here is Stephen Leacock using the bare bones of the opposite:

> [The salesman] should select from his wardrobe a suit of plain, severe design, attractive and yet simple, good and yet bad, long and at the same time short, in other words something that is expensive but cheap.

Here is Stephen Leacock using an opposite with more clay:

> With the aid of four stakes driven deeply into the ground and with blankets strung upon them, I managed to fashion a sort of rude tent, roofless, but otherwise quite sheltered.

Shortly after I began writing prose humor, and heavily under the influence of Lewis Carroll's way of dressing up bare opposites, as in this example:

> The sun was shining on the sea,
> Shining with all his might . . .
> And this was odd, because it was
> The middle of the night.

I decided to write some humorous verse and thus increase my

income. My first attempt consisted of throwing together every
bare opposite I could think of:

> I found a brand new insect,
> But no matter how I tried,
> I could not see him long enough
> To get him classified.
>
> His legs are either four or six,
> I think that he has wings,
> But the strangest thing about him
> Is the curious way he sings.
>
> He makes a noise that has no sound,
> And thus cannot be heard;
> It's like the sound that no one makes
> When no one says a word.
>
> To produce this eerie silence
> His two hind legs are raised,
> And then his call (no sound at all)
> Leaves everyone amazed.
>
> Just what he does to make no buzz,
> I cannot say for sure;
> I did not have my glasses
> And the light was very poor.
>
> I know he used his legs, but I
> Could not determine whether
> It was done by holding them apart
> Or rubbing them together.
>
> My notes on him are not complete
> And it never may be clear

Just how he sings this song I was
The first one not to hear.*

In dressing up a bare opposite there must be enough elaboration to introduce convincingness. It need not be much, since only the subconscious mind need be convinced, and the subconscious mind is not overly shrewd. But it must be there.

In commenting on his advancing age Robert Benchley said that he had noticed that his knees would bend backward as easily as forward. This is good enough for the subconscious mind, who is aware that lots of things bend back and forth and that knees sometimes become a little unreliable with age.

James Branch Cabell has one of his characters say: "Plainly the tide is coming in. Or else it is going out."

The subconscious mind is aware that the tide goes in and out. Possibly at the same time. He will check this with the conscious mind. The conscious mind sees the false logic but it is too late. One has already laughed.

A superior paradox, such as this one by Oliver Wendell Holmes: "Give us the luxuries of life, and we will dispense with its necessities," depends on the opposite of transposing words to opposite positions, and shares the same basic structure as such metatheses as "Pardon me, madam, you are occupewing the wrong pie. I will sew you to another sheet," and "I have had only tea martoonies," and the urging of a radio announcer to "visit your nearest A and Poo Feed Store," which depend on the opposite of transposing syllables.

Oscar Wilde was fond of opposites and was constantly saying things like: "I do not approve of anything that tampers with natural ignorance," which sounds all right to the subconscious mind until he examines it more carefully.

*Reprinted with permission from *The Saturday Evening Post,* © 1949 The Curtis Publishing Company.

6

The Opposite

To call a waitress who is dressed in a white dress and a white hat by saying "Nurse!" is a visual pun, and is an opposite in the sense that the waitress may be called a non-nurse. In the same way someone who imitates Barbra Streisand may be called a non-Streisand. A word that imitates another word is the same kind of opposite.

To put the emphasis in the wrong place means that there is a nonemphasis where the emphasis should be and it is therefore an opposite. The positions are reversed more or less in the same manner that the positions of two words may be reversed in a paradox. Thus "A martyr is a pile of wood set on fire with a man on top" can be considered to be an opposite, and so can "Will you give me a penny, mister? I haven't eaten for three days and I want to weigh myself."

When Oscar Wilde heard something sad, he remarked: "I'm very much affected." To which James McNeill Whistler replied: "You certainly are." Groucho Marx takes the opposite meaning from "There's a man outside with a black moustache," when he says, "Tell him I've got one." The same kind of opposite occurs when a man says to his new secretary, "There are two words I must ask you never to use in my presence. One of them is 'lousy,' the other is 'swell,' " and she replies, "All right. What are the two words?"

An ellipsis may be called an opposite on the ground that the absence of something and the presence of something else constitute an opposite, as illustrated by this bit, written by a child:

When my father was about fifteen he sold meat from a wagon. One day a girl asked him for a piece of baloney which later proved to be my mother.

7

Any behavior opposite to accepted behavior is considered to be amusing, as for example that of a man who purchases live bait and gives it its freedom. Dickens made use of this principle in "The Boarding House":

> The next morning being Sunday, breakfast was laid in the front parlor at ten o'clock . . . Tibbs enrobed himself in his Sunday costume . . . and mounted to the parlor aforesaid. Nobody had come down, and he amused himself by drinking the contents of the milkpot with a teaspoon.

One can break down the opposite into categories such as resentment of authority, much-to-do-little, puns, and so on, and then, for example, separate written puns from visual puns, and further break down visual puns into categories which do not exist but can be named, such as Pretending a Thing is What it Appears to Be, which can itself be broken down into other subcategories to include such things as one person's imitation of another, or the accidental resemblance of a cloud formation to one's aunt. There is, in fact, no end to categories if one chooses to make them. But all of them are types of the opposite.

2

Exaggeration

One of the inconveniences of the English language is that it assigns specific meanings to words. This sometimes restricts one's ability to make one's meaning clear. For example it is forbidden to use the word "square" to mean "oblong." If one could speak of degrees of squareness one would not need the word "oblong" at all, and one could form a theory beginning "All tables are square (with the exception of round tables, which includes oval tables)."

In presenting a theory that all humor is based on an opposite I must be permitted to speak of degrees of oppositeness so as to include exaggeration, which is a kind of opposite just as an oblong is a kind of square. The more extreme the exaggeration the more it approaches the opposite of the reader's belief.

An opposite may be defined as two ideas 180 degrees apart, and an extreme exaggeration may be defined as two ideas 170 degrees apart. Both attack the reader's judgment. The attack must be violent. The opposite represents a completely opposing view to that which the reader holds, and the exaggeration is far away from what the reader believes. Nothing else is violent enough to be used as a basis for humor.

Exaggeration is not necessarily funny. A thought must be given form and convincingness, and be composed into a whole, before it can be made funny. The attack must be made extreme and the escape from being fooled, the false logic, carefully calculated. The reader is aware that there are shades of correctness and arguable points. Within those margins he is not so much being attacked as consulted. The difficulty of correcting a misspelled word may be a joint effort.

If the reader is presented with an opposite or an exaggeration of something he believes, in such a convincing manner that it appears to his subconscious mind to be capable of destroying his belief, he rejects the idea with laughter. The false logic is inserted by the humorist so that it will be seen, and the convincingness is inserted by the humorist so that the idea will need rejection.

In composing a piece of humor one begins by choosing a subject familiar to the audience and reduces a part of that subject to a statement of fact. This statement of fact is equivalent to a truth, or something accepted as true, a cliché, or any common belief or knowledge. One then either twists the statement into an opposite, or carries the idea to an extreme.

In the case of exaggeration vanity might be the general subject and, although I hate to bring myself into it, "I am handsome" might be the statement of fact. One then exaggerates the basic statement, as I have done in this verse:

> In spite of a wen
> Ever since I was ten
> My appearance is perfectly charming;

Exaggeration

And the way it affects
The opposite sex
I can only describe as alarming.

They shriek and they squeal;
They ask if I'm real;
They ask are my eyelashes false;
When I say, "No, they ain't,"
Quite a few of them faint,
While others require smelling salts.

I suppose that one might
Say my looks are just right,
For I haven't a single bad feature;
I have studied them all
And I'm what you'd call
A beautiful, breath-taking creature.

My nose and my ears
Bring spontaneous cheers;
My chin is quite firm and well-rounded;
With my face in full view,
There are cries of, "Yoo-hoo!"
While my profile leaves people astounded.

When seen from the right
I could scream with delight;
My profile is noble, serene;
But I take equal pride
In my gorgeous left side;
I'm confused, if you see what I mean.

But I should make it plain
That I'm not the least vain,
And the fact that I'm handsome just bores me;

As does all the clamor
From the girls who love glamor
Each one of whom simply adores me.*

The greatest extreme that one can think of is always the strongest and funniest, provided one has contrived by some means to make the exaggeration convincing for the short time it takes the reader to see the point and laugh.

This is true of any exaggeration, whether in writing or drawing. Whatever it is, it becomes progressively funnier as it approaches the greatest believable extreme, and progressively less funny as it passes the greatest believable extreme.

For example, when one caricatures a large nose one makes the nose larger. Whatever humor there is in a nose becomes greater and then less as the nose becomes larger, until one reaches the point at which the reader is totally unconvinced that such a nose could exist. His judgment is no longer attacked and there is nothing to reject. A nose that extends all the way across a room has no humor at all.

Stephen Leacock is well aware of the limits of exaggeration and is guided by them in making his decision as to just how dilapidated to make his salesman:

The well-dressed man—in selling, let us say, municipal bonds—has an initial advantage over the man who comes into his customer's store in tattered rags, with his toes protruding from his boots, unshaved and with a general air of want and misery stamped all over him. Customers are quick to notice these little things.

Exaggeration

The limit of exaggeration was also reached by the Comte de Marachal, who was so proud of his pedigree that he had a picture of the Flood painted showing a man running after Noah, saying: "My good friend, save the archives of the Marachal family!"

Voltaire uses pedigree as the subject of exaggeration when Candide's mother refuses to marry a man "because he could only prove seventy-two quarterings," the rest of his genealogical tree being lost.

Whether one consciously begins with a basic statement or not, the basic statement is implicitly there. If George is the subject, the basic statement may be "George walks funny," or "George uses too many gestures." One always has a choice of what facet of a subject to exaggerate. In an imitation of George one might choose to exaggerate his manner of speaking or of wearing his hat.

In exaggerating the cliché "It's a dry heat so you don't feel it so much," one would seek to place two characters in the hottest setting one could think of. The characters might be two stokers shoveling coal into the boilers of a ship, or two devils in hell.

Both the opposite and the exaggeration are attempts to fool the reader. This attempt is defeated and defeated quickly. If there is too long a delay the attack is too successful. The reader does not reject the idea because he sees nothing wrong with it. On the other hand, if the false logic is so feeble that it is seen through without any delay there is no reason to laugh because self-justification is not involved. The humorist must teeter along, striking a balance between convincingness and exaggeration.

He begins with convincingness. "Kansas is flat." The reader agrees. He has heard about that. The reader also accepts the second line, "Kansas is not perfectly flat, as some people suppose." This sounds judicious. The reader agrees that some people tend to exaggerate, and begins to feel that he is in the presence of a reasonable man who would not fool him. The next sentence has a reassuring statistical sound: "There is a drop of seven feet per mile from the western edge to the eastern edge."

Since the first three sentences have struck the reader as being perfectly reasonable, he rather expects the fourth sentence to be reasonable as well. The first glimpse of the meaning of what someone is saying is like our own intention of saying something before we say it. We have a dawning sense of where the words spoken thus far will lead. But the fourth sentence does not lead there: "A marble, placed on the western edge, would roll all the way across to Missouri."

With this piece of false logic the writer has gained the important split-second delay. The reader, who agrees that Kansas is flat, is presented with the problem of distinguishing between "level" and "flat" at the same moment he hears about this marble.

The balance between exaggeration and convincingness can vary greatly. Thomas Hardy is heavy on convincingness. In his novel, *The Trumpet Major,* the heroine, Anne,

> lived with her widowed mother in a portion of an ancient building formerly a manor-house, but now a mill, which being too large for his own requirements, the miller had found it convenient to divide and appropriate in part to these highly respectable tenants. In this dwelling Mrs. Garland's and Anne's ears were soothed morning, noon and night by the music of the mill, the wheels and cogs of which, being of wood, produced notes that might have

borne in their minds a remote resemblance to the wooden tones of the stopped diapason in an organ. Occasionally, when the miller was bolting, there was added to these continuous sounds the cheerful clicking of the hopper, which did not deprive them of rest except when it was kept going all night; and over and above all this they had the pleasure of knowing that there crept in through every crevice, door, and window of their dwelling, however tightly closed, a subtle mist of superfine flour from the grinding-room, quite invisible, but making its presence known in the course of time by giving a pallid and ghastly look to the best furniture.

Voltaire, on the other hand, is heavy on exaggeration and light on convincingness. Mr. Micromegas, an inhabitant of the star Sirius, is "120,000 royal feet tall" and fifty thousand feet around the waist. His nose is 6,333 feet long. In his 670th year he travels to improve his education. Traveling through space he lands on the planet Saturn and is amused at the small size of the inhabitants, who are only 6,000 feet tall. Micromegas wonders how, with only seventy-two senses, they can ever know reality:

"To what age do you commonly live?"
"Alas! Few, very few on this globe outlive 500 revolutions around the sun (these, according to our way of reckoning, amount to about 15,000 years). So you see, we in a manner begin to die the very moment we are born. . . . Scarce do we learn a little when death intervenes before we can profit by experience."

The exaggeration of dimensions used by Voltaire would

not ordinarily be accepted. In order to achieve momentary convincingness he places the 120,000-feet-tall people on another planet.

The device of repeating a word or phrase unnecessarily is sometimes an effective form of exaggeration. Dickens used the device in "The Tuggs at Ramsgate," at a point in the story at which a man arrives from a commercial establishment called the Temple, with some money for the Tuggs family:

> "I come from the Temple," said the man with the bag.
>
> "From the Temple!" said Mrs. Tuggs, flinging open the door and disclosing Miss Tuggs in perspective.
>
> "From the Temple!" said Miss Tuggs and Mr. Cymon Tuggs at the same moment.
>
> "From the Temple!" said Mr. Joseph Tuggs, turning as pale as a Dutch cheese.
>
> "From the Temple," repeated the man with the bag.

The trick, as with all exaggeration, is to know when to stop.

3

The Subconscious

I like this chapter title. It has the sound of raw scholarship. But I am afraid that the intellectual people who turned at once to this chapter, ignoring all the other chapters, will be disappointed. I know almost nothing about psychiatry.

However, I do know how my own subconscious mind works. It is like another person inside me. When I go to sleep he remains awake, watching for enemies. He uses my nose. If he smells gas he awakens me at once. He uses my ears. I can't hear anything, but he can. If he hears any suspicious noises he awakens me at once. He is unable to use my eyes because I sleep with them closed.

It is even possible to communicate directly with him, and to give him instructions which he will follow carefully. If the reader doubts this let him try it for himself. Direct your subconscious mind to awaken you at 7:30 and he will awaken you at 7:30. Six-thirty if you are on daylight saving time.

Fifteen million years ago it was his custom while I was asleep on the ground to remain alert, using my nose to sniff the jungle air (which involved his using the most ancient part of the cerebral cortex) , and twitching my ears nervously (using muscles that I have since lost) , in order to catch the first faint sign of any tigers creeping up on me through the bushes.

He is still there, with his unchanged neuron circuits, protecting me to the best of his ability. There are no tigers in New York City, and the poor fellow has learned not to bother me for ordinary traffic noises, no matter how loud. However, two people discussing innocent matters in low tones on the sidewalk beneath my window sound to him conspiratorial.

"When we sneak in," he imagines them saying, "you hold him down, and I'll hit him."

He awakens me at once.

He remembers tigers clearly and is somewhat suspicious that there may still be a few around. But the driving force of life is to adjust. He has had to transfer his tiger work to modern times. Intelligence has evolved and it is now my self-esteem that needs his protection and not my body.

Through his connections he has learned that I fear attacks on my knowledge and judgment. He sees this as a new land full of new enemies. When I am engaged in conversation he keeps his ears pricked, alert for anything creeping up on me through the verbiage. At the first sign of danger he sends a message to my conscious mind:

"We are being attacked! By what, I don't know."

"Remain calm," says my conscious mind. "It is merely a paradox. I can handle it."

The primary function of the brain is to protect us from harm. The prehistoric jungle was savage beyond our comprehension. No matter which way one turned one ran into a tiger. There were twenty separate and distinct species, each of them delighted to have a prehominid for dinner if he could catch one.

The subconscious mind is proud of the job he did in those days. He protected us from bodily harm so successfully that we are here today. Now he has been transferred to another department. He regards his new assignment as being just as important as his tiger work. Indeed, he makes no distinction between the two. As far as he is concerned, an attack on the mind is just as serious as an attack on the body. For this reason he peers behind each sentence as he used to peer behind each tree.

The subconscious mind works deep in the recesses of memory and recognition. He has at his command millions of neural paths containing a gallimaufry of semireliable information. Some brain paths are not very deeply etched. On being introduced to someone a tiny brain path makes a note of the name. While you talk of other things the brain path slowly fills in, like a crease made with a knife in soft fudge. Nothing is left except a slight indication of the crease at one end, which is the letter "B." You know his name begins with "B," and that's all you know.

The associative brain path you took the trouble to etch, bearing the additional information that his name, Banyard, closely resembles the word "barnyard," by a further association makes you think his name is "Chickenhouse," which is worse than having no memory path at all.

As one listens to the story about the dog which dashed back into the burning house and returned with the insurance papers wrapped in a damp towel, the subconscious mind is busy shuffling the molecules in his memory bank, and flipping through the lantern slides in his file labelled "visual images."

Having found what he wants the subconscious mind merely

19

turns an electrical switch which starts the frontal lobes clacking together, and presently a series of lantern slides, some of them rather badly smudged, pass in rapid succession through the conscious mind, showing dogs, fires, and towels. Since words are merely symbols for abstractions, each listener sees a different dog, fire, and towel.

At the same time there is a rapid and continuous comparison of one's knowledge with the facts being presented. A constant supply of bits of memory surrounds each word of the story, confirming or denying its truth. At first there is no shock from any incongruity. One has heard of the remarkable intelligence of animals, of course.

As the story proceeds the subconscious mind narrows his eyes and listens carefully for anything "not right." When insurance papers are mentioned the subconscious mind closes a switch which causes the frontal lobes to throb. One appears to be confronted with a statement contrary to one's belief. One had always understood that dogs were unable to read. How then had the dog selected insurance papers from among others?

When we are told that the dog wrapped the insurance papers in a damp towel we check the lantern slides again, choosing one showing a dog standing on his hind legs at the washbasin in a bathroom. He is holding the towel in one paw and turning on the water with the other. The insurance papers are in his mouth. The image is unacceptable. It is rejected with laughter.

4

Laughter

I have no hesitation in saying that laughter is a modification of the noise that used to frighten tigers away. Any theory on the cause of laughter must explain why laughter is vocal. Further, it must explain why the vocal elements take the peculiar reiterated form they do. Why the mouth is opened to the point, but not beyond the point, that will allow the loudest noise. Why the vocal chords are held as tense as possible, while inarticulate sounds from the vibrating larynx and pharynx are combined with a series of expiratory blasts, emitting the loud clear sound of *Ha! Ha! Ha!* Why laughter stimulates respiration and circulation, raises the blood pressure, and sends a larger supply of blood to the brain, as if one was about to climb a tree. Finally, why, when one analyzes the feeling of triumph that follows laughter, one finds it to be colored with a feeling of deliverance from danger.

Nature does not invent reactions unnecessarily, so I suspect that fifteen million years ago Og saw a tiger creeping toward him and uttered a loud noise which caused the tiger to veer off into the bushes. Six months later Guk was trotting through the green gloom of a jungle trail and came upon a tiger with foot-long teeth. Remembering what Og had told him, Guk opened his mouth and uttered a loud noise, whereupon the tiger bounded off into the forest.

It became generally known that when attacked by a tiger it was a good idea to make a loud noise. It worked 50 percent of the time, and we are descended from people who ran across nervous tigers. As a direct descendant of Og, I can tell you that he was not killed until after he had children.

It is well known that laughter is contagious, which for the purposes of this theory simply means that when other members of the tribe heard Og trying to drive a tiger away they all raised their voices to help drive the tiger away. Today, when the subconscious mind listens to the Laughing Record, it sounds to him as if somebody is trying to drive a tiger away and he joins in.

The tiger noise wore a deep brain path which we have inherited. Since there are very few tigers around, the noise has been adapted for use in other ways. It has become a tool that can be used for something else, just as your wife's scissors can be used to pry the lid off a paint can.

The air sac used by the crossopterygian fish to keep himself at any desired depth in the water was adapted for use in breathing when he crawled out on land. The automobile horn whose original use was to let people know that an automobile was coming, having outlived that purpose since there is always an automobile coming, is now used to tell people that the light is about to change.

Laughter is an inherited protective device which, since it is still handy, has been pressed into service for a variety of uses. It has been modified in such a way that it is useful even against small attacks. One can now adjust one's laughter to the seriousness of the attack. The sound that sent tigers away has become the sound that sends puns away.

To state baldly what the humorist does sounds almost un-friendly. The humorist sets out to make the reader look like a fool. But only because this is a necessary part of the humor structure. The humorist's real motive is to bring pleasure to the reader. In order to do so he must make the reader laugh. In order to make him laugh he must attack the reader's judgment or knowledge. The laughter will be followed by pleasure, the reader having repelled the attack. He will have a comfortable feeling of renewed security. He is not to be eaten after all.

Because the attack must be violent the humorist uses either an opposite or an exaggeration as the base of the attack because they are furthest removed from what the reader believes. Seeing the point of a joke, or seeing the point of any humor structure, may be compared to seeing the tiger. If one sees the point of a joke there is a split second of stark horror, after which one laughs, repelling the attack on one's mental body, and this is followed instantly by pleasure. If one does not see the point of a joke one is eaten.

The hearer of a joke laughs, the teller does not. There is a tiger present. The teller of the joke has already seen the tiger and cannot be surprised. When he first saw the tiger, or the point of the joke, he laughed. Now he is going to point out the tiger to the second person. When the point of the joke is reached the hearer laughs. He sees the tiger being pointed out to him. He gets the point.

The teller now joins in the laughter, because of the old idea that if one heard the tiger noise one joined in to help drive the tiger away, and because he is again visualizing the tiger, and because the tiger noise has developed into a sign used in any association with the tiger. A pathway had been formed in the brain, and the current of association of ideas and memory concerning the tiger tended to escape by the same pathway from then on. It is easier to fold a paper that has been folded already.

When one has been through a danger there is an impulse to tell people about it. One has been in jeopardy and retelling the story diffuses the feeling of fear.

"What happened?" people ask anxiously. "How awful! How did you escape?"

One gets lots of sympathy, which is exactly what one needed when one faced the tiger, and one gets lots of credit for having escaped.

Fifteen million years ago we did not yet have fire. But as the prehominids gathered of an evening in a circle around the point where the fire would have been if they had had one, there was always someone who would make himself the center of attention with his stories of narrow escapes from tigers.

When the story of his adventures reached the point at which the tiger sprang from the bushes, each member of the audience greeted the appearance of the tiger with the appropriate tiger noise, those with the greatest power of visualization laughing the loudest.

There was also the prehominid who could not remember any stories about tigers, which is the same thing as forgetting jokes. Once the tiger was gone he never thought about it again.

In those days as in these, some people told a story better than others. I am acquainted with a vice-president of an investment firm who wonders why he isn't president. It's very simple. The poor sap tells a joke backward. He says: "Did I tell you the joke about the two Texans who were buying a car and one of them said, 'No, no. Let me pay for it. You paid for the lunch?' . . . No? Well, it seems these two Texans were having lunch. . . ."

His ancestor told a story the same way. "Did I tell you about Thurg going down to the water hole for a drink and this tiger jumped at him from the top of a boulder, but Thurg jumped into the water and got away? . . . No? Well. . . ."

The point of a joke has its full effect only if it comes as a surprise to the hearer. Surprise in general is not necessarily funny. One must be surprised by a tiger. The joke must be new to the hearer. If he has already seen the tiger there is no surprise. If he already knows the joke he sees the tiger coming a long way off. He need only give the grunt that has become the symbolic acknowledgment that there is a tiger in the vicinity.

Tickling, which represents an attack by an animal, is accompanied by violent body movements. One jumps around and squirms trying to get free. One is totally helpless in the hands of a real tickler. There is a feeling of extreme danger. One laughs continuously in an effort to frighten away the attacker. Tears stream down the cheeks, one gasps and can't get one's breath. Even in the hands of a kindly uncle the squirming is fundamentally a struggle to remove an enemy, and the laughter fundamentally an attempt to frighten the enemy away.

The laughter of play also stems from the instinct for self-preservation and has to do with the instinctive acquisition of skills useful in hunting, fighting, and flight. It has been modified to combine the noise used to frighten tigers away with a habit of laughter formed in childhood expressing pleasure.

Modifications of Laughter

One must draw a distinct line between the laughter caused by pleasure and the laughter caused by a humor structure. They are two quite different things and represent two quite different emotions, just as the tears shed on hearing a beautiful construction of music are quite different from the tears shed on hitting one's thumb with a hammer.

When we laugh at humor there is a tiger present. When we laugh from pleasure there is no tiger. Hilarity at the next table in a restaurant does not necessarily mean that anyone at the table has composed a masterpiece of humor. What is going on is high spirits, not art.

One might assume that if one is already feeling pleasure, if everything is going well, one would be inclined to be gay and would laugh at a humor structure one would not laugh at in a somber mood. I deny this. But I do not deny that under exactly the same happy circumstances one might laugh aloud from sheer pleasure.

I think that pleasure has nothing to do with the cause of laughter at humor for the same reason I am of the opinion that superiority has nothing to do with the cause of laughter at humor. Either or both may be present but one laughs at humor to defend oneself against the attack of an opposite accompanied by convincingness.

Prehistoric laughter became so intimately associated with the pleasure of seeing the tiger depart that it has become a sign of pleasure in general. Shaking the head from side to side, originally in the refusal of food, has become a sign of negation in general. The frown, originally useful to keep the eyes from being engorged with blood while screaming, has become a sign of displeasure in general.

Laughter

The smile, or perhaps the laugh of pleasure, expresses satisfaction with things as they are. The laughter of pleasure never reaches the point of helpless paroxysm, the bull-like bellow, the gasping, and the beet-red face that is sometimes the reaction to a piece of humor. This requires a tiger. Self-preservation is involved.

In a reaction involving self-preservation adrenalin is poured into the blood, the blood pressure rises, forcing more blood into the muscles, lungs, and brain as a preparation for fighting or for flight. Sugar is mobilized for the production of energy, the coagulability of the blood is increased so that wounds about to be received will be less likely to be fatal. This is hardly a description of a feeling of pleasure but very much a description of what happens physically in violent laughter at humor.

It is difficult to show the separation of an emotional condition such as pleasure from an instinctive reaction such as laughter at humor, especially when both are expressed in more or less the same way and can be expressed at the same time. One's mind is able to accommodate more than one reaction at the same time, as in the case of being clapped heartily on the sunburn as the point of a joke is reached. But the two reactions are separate, and the pain of sunburn has nothing to do with the cause of laughter.

Laughter at humor depends on self-love. One's personality is sacred. One wavers between pride and shame depending on how well instinct and the conscious mind act together in maintaining the self. Emotion appears when there is a threat to self-satisfaction. Laughter at humor produces pleasure because a danger has been removed.

Superiority has often been advanced as a cause of laughter, but it is not precise to call this sense of security, this successful

27

defense of self-esteem, a feeling of superiority. It is a feeling of safety. The feeling of deliverance from danger that accompanies laughter at humor affects the center of the instinct for self-preservation, which is found in the neuron circuits inherited from our prehominid ancestor of fifteen million years ago.

The classic situation in which superiority is assumed to be the cause of laughter can be summed up in the sentence "He did it, I did not," and can be made more specific: "He hit the golf ball into the cornfield, I did not. He fell down, I did not. He misused a word, I did not." When this kind of complication of a piece of humor is completed, superiority may be present but it is not the cause of laughter.

If the seven colors of the rainbow are put on a color wheel and spun, one sees only white. When the separate parts of a piece of humor are joined together and made into a whole thing, the humor structure, that is to say the opposite with its convincingness, is not always easy to distinguish, but it is there separate and alone as a cause of laughter. It is the tiger, hidden in the verbiage, that one defends oneself against.

Character, setting, subject matter, and style may be represented by other colors. Superiority, aggression, egotism, guilt, anxiety, jealousy, or truth may be present, but none of these is the cause of laughter. If the humor structure is removed there is nothing to laugh at.

If superiority is present it does not mean that one has feelings of superiority. If two men swim away from a foundered boat and one reaches the shore and the other drowns, the feelings of the saved man are those of thankfulness for the preservation of self. He is superior to the other man. He swims better than the other man. The other man drowned, he did not. But he has no feelings of superiority.

If one draws a cartoon of a man walking into the offices of

the Internal Revenue Service, with the caption, "I would like to speak to somebody soft-hearted," there are both sympathy and superiority present. Sympathy because we have been in the same sort of uncomfortable position. Superiority because he is in the uncomfortable position, we are not.

But neither of these is the cause of laughter. We laugh because the cliché, "There are no soft-hearted people in the Internal Revenue Service," has been made into an opposite. It is the same kind of opposite that one might use in an attempt to fool one's companion by raising one finger and calling, "Taxi!" during a taxi strike. There are no taxis.

Pleasure is simply one more color on the color wheel. It may or may not be present. If pleasure is already present when one hears a joke, one may laugh from pleasure at the same time one laughs at the joke. But the amount of laughter caused by feeling pleasure is separate and distinct from the amount of laughter caused by the joke. They are not seen as two separate reactions because the color wheel has been spun.

Pleasure may be present in the same way that superiority or aggression may be present, none of them having anything whatever to do with the cause of laughter at humor. If the humor structure is removed one is left sitting there feeling aggressive and superior, and smiling or laughing with pleasure, and nothing else. It seems to me.

What makes this slightly confusing is the fact that pleasure exists in both cases. In the case of laughter at humor pleasure arises on seeing the tiger depart. Pleasure follows laughter so closely that they seem to occur simultaneously. But they do not occur simultaneously. No pleasure is felt until one sees the tiger veer off, frightened by the noise of laughter. In the laughter of pleasure there is no tiger. There is no feeling of having escaped danger. Neither is the sudden relief from the cares of life, or the situation that arouses the childish laugh of sheer pleasure, necessarily funny, or accompanied by a feeling of triumph.

The modification of laughter has resulted in the gradation of laughter. One's laughter is adjusted to the degree of danger represented by the attack, so that a small joke is rejected with a small laugh.

One's reaction to humor is instinctive and essentially involuntary, so that laughter can be imitated only imperfectly. But it can be imitated. Both the loud laugh and the small laugh can be used for social purposes.

Usually the subconscious mind sees the problem, the intelligence solves it. In the case of the social laugh it is the intelligence that sees the problem. The problem is to get to be vice-president of the company. The intelligence also solves the problem with an extremely cultivated loud laugh that is turned on wherever it will do the most good. This is the same laugh used by the people in the sycophant business.

The social laugh does not necessarily mean that one is feeling either amusement or pleasure. It is merely a sign of self-assurance. It is a signal that one is successful and not depressed.

The man who skulks into a room with a depressed look on his face is not likely to be thought of as successful, unless he is someone like Oscar Levant who made a life's work of it. The man who walks into the room with a flushed, healthy face, rubbing his hands together and laughing, is portraying well-being, based on the truth that a person who is in good spirits is often successful. The performance has been noted and copied by people who try to portray well-being based on success by wearing fake diamonds and fake alligator shoes.

There is also a social laugh which is quite acceptable and

merely good manners. Laughing and crying have been conditioned to express appropriate social attitudes. One has learned that by weeping and saying, "Ah, the poor fellow!" one can communicate to others the idea that one has adopted the proper social attitude. Smiling can be used in the same way as an obligatory expression of certain emotions whether one feels them or not.

When your hostess tells you that you are going to love Algy and Harriet there is a certain social obligation to live up to. You may have no genuine feeling for the hostess, and even less for the miserable creatures you are going to meet, but when the moment comes you put your best foot forward and present your best self. You do not fall on the floor and froth at the mouth, or mumble that you will be outside. You prepare your face with a smile. You tell them that you have heard so much about them, at the same time you try to think what it was, and that you so much admire his work in linoleum. The situation requires one to be charming and personable, and the accepted signal is the smile.

The smile is essentially an expression of the pleasure of satisfied hunger. While its origin obviously goes back a long way, it does not go back to the same thing as the laughter at humor. It has nothing to do with the vocal elements of laughter, and laughter is basically vocal.

The smile is silent and associated with pleasure, either real or assumed, and not infrequently appears as an expression of satisfaction at any success, such as knocking all ten pins down at bowling. The smile is also a convention used to acknowledge that an attempt at humor has been made, but so weakly that it does not deserve a laugh.

There is the smile of anticipation. But there is a sharp line between the smile that anticipates pleasure and the smile that anticipates the danger of being told a joke. Anticipation rather than retrospection was probably the most important primitive function of ideas. The up-and-coming prehominid spent more time looking for a tiger behind the next bend in the trail than he did thinking about the tiger he had escaped the previous week.

When approaching a bend in the trail, or a favorite comedian, one may smile. One has been in this part of the forest before and one knows that tigers abound. It pays to be ready. One prepares one's mouth for instant laughter. On going to meet a compatible friend there may also be a smile of anticipation. The meeting of such a friend implies many past happy experiences and the anticipation of another. But one does not anticipate any tigers. It is well known that there are no tigers in the vicinity. The greatest danger one will meet with is an aphorism.

5

Getting the Point

Getting the point of a joke corresponds to seeing the tiger. Of course it is no longer the same thing. Our reaction to seeing the tiger has been modified over a period of millions of years. Hearing a good joke is much more fun than being attacked by a tiger. Not only has the sound we call laughter changed. Our reaction is no longer such a simple one.

Pleasure has become identified with laughter, instinct has become mixed with intelligence. The whole sequence of surprise, laughter, triumph, and pleasure has been transferred from one thing to another. It has become something else. The process has changed in the way a dolphin's hand has changed. Hidden inside the dolphin's flipper are all the bones of the hand, including all the small bones of the five fingers.

Our reaction on seeing the point of a joke is greater when the point of the joke comes as a surprise. We laugh harder. Seeing a tiger in the distance, or seeing the point of a joke in the distance, does not represent a great danger. It is not necessary to make the tiger noise or to laugh.

If the point of a joke is too obvious the reader will give a hollow laugh to announce that he sees the point. If the point of a joke is too obscure, if in effect there is no tiger to be seen anywhere, he will not laugh at all. Self-justification is not involved because none of his friends would get the point either. In the first case there is no reason to laugh at getting the point because it is too easy, and in the second case because it is too hard.

A split-second delay in getting the point of a joke is cleverly arranged by the clever humorist so that the audience he is writing to will expend a certain small amount of psychic energy, no more and no less. An example of perfection is Anthony Trollope's description of his character Mr. Slope, who "had added an 'e' to his name for the sake of euphony."

You get what you pay for. More psychic energy is required by Muggeridge than by Mutt and Jeff. If your life has been reasonably profound you will get more out of Muggeridge than will a barber who has been reading *Mad* magazine for twenty years.

The thing to be done by the humorist is to make getting the point just difficult enough so that the reader must laugh in order to feel triumph and pleasure. One is fooled only for a split second, and fortunately it is only necessary to fool the subconscious mind, who thinks that anybody whispering on the sidewalk is going to attack me, and who thinks that the imitator of Streisand may be Streisand herself, while one's intelligence knows from the very beginning that it is not Streisand.

Our intelligence recognizes the precise character of the point of a joke. Our awareness of attack and the laughter it causes are the business of the subconscious mind. The poor fellow is easily fooled for that split second and is constantly pressing one of his electrical knobs to tell us that someone is walking on the ceiling, which is an opposite to our belief, but that he has glue on his feet, which is convincingness. At that point the intelligence takes over. But the fact that we have successfully repulsed an attack is not necessarily explicitly recognized.

Humor requires a certain amount of attention. Habit diminishes the amount of attention, so that people intending only to change their shoes have been known to continue undressing and get into bed. Systems of reflex paths in the brain wake each other up successively. At the clue of the first part of a sentence electrical impulses begin zipping from one neuron to another, activating association of ideas, memory, and reasoning. Since one has heard it before, the memory image makes anticipation possible. When one reads:

> One misty, moisty morning
> When cloudy was the weather,
> The official forecast was
> Fair and warmer.

one's thought is so swift that before one can stop it it has rushed to a conclusion. It is the wrong conclusion, and is like not paying attention on a jungle trail and suddenly being confronted by a tiger.

The element of surprise, or the split second, cannot be measured exactly. Some brains revolve more slowly than others, and the humorist who desires a broad audience will sometimes deliberately construct a piece of humor so that the quick-witted members of the audience and Nature's slow thinkers will both get the point of the joke at the precise moment necessary to make them laugh, although the length of the split-second delay will vary.

For example, the curtain rises to reveal a seated character holding a book upside down. Some members of the audience laugh, having already observed that the book is upside down, and having already got the point: the character is unable to read.

For the benefit of those members of the audience whose split-second time is longer the author has written some dialogue:

"What are you doing?"

"I'm reading."

"You're holding the book upside down."

At this point the rest of the audience laughs.

Professor Wilhelm Wundt conducted a reaction-time experiment which he called "Untershiedungszeit." The experiment was well named, and consisted of the sudden appearance of a black or white object. The average reaction times of three subjects were, in seconds, 0.050, 0.047, and 0.079.

Professor James Cattell found he could get no results by this method, and preferred an experiment which Wundt called the "einfache Wahlmethode." This too I think is a good name for an experiment. Using the einfache Wahlmethode, Professor Cattell got results of 0.030 and 0.050.

Reaction time to the sudden appearance of an unforeseen word turned out to be 5/6 of a second.

In a piece of humor the presentation of problem and solution is almost simultaneous. Almost, but not quite. There is almost no difficulty in getting the point, and you have been made to feel clever. But there is some difficulty. You have to do some work. You do have to apprehend. The expenditure of energy is exact. It is a small but exact amount.

If someone tells you that God is a woman you begin to consider the matter carefully. There is no split second of delay while you get the point. But if a woman says, "Put your faith in God, She will protect you," it is considered to be a joke. There is a point to get. There is a split second of delay while one transposes the joke to the basic statement, "God is a woman."

Of course getting a point is not necessarily funny. There must be a humor idea to begin with and there must be a split second delay expertly timed. The technique employed by the humorist in arranging something for the audience to get is to begin with a flat statement, transpose it to something that says the same thing, and allow the audience to transpose it again to the original flat statement.

The statement "This man cannot read" is transposed by the humorist by showing a book held upside down, which is transposed by the audience to "This man cannot read."

The statement "Women are not good bowlers" is transposed by the cartoonist by showing a pin boy approaching a woman bowler and saying, "If you knock anything over, call me."

The flat statement that a woman is a bad cook is not funny. Transposed, as by the husband saying, "What's in this, dear? I may have to describe it to a doctor," it gains the valuable split-second delay while the audience transposes it to the original basic statement, "The woman is a bad cook."

At a birthday party, one guest observing a cake with thirty-nine candles might remark to another guest, "She's certainly older than that!" The other guest might smile in agreement because of the mild opposite involved. But there is no split second delay, nothing to get, and no transposition necessary. The split second delay is added when the guest says to the woman whose birthday it is, "I count only thirty-nine candles. Are they being continued on another cake?"

It might be argued that one might expect a feeling of satisfaction on seeing the point of a joke without all this speculation about tigers. But this does not explain laughter. Most especially it does not explain why laughter is vocal. Why a loud noise must precede this kind of satisfaction. The ordinary intellectual accomplishment, while it may bring satisfaction, does not necessarily cause laughter. Getting the point, as a part of a humor structure, has in it an echo of the past.

6

A Sense of Humor

The laughter of a child is unprogrammed, genuine, and brand new. All of the forms and the techniques of humor are responded to. A sixty-year-old knows what he is supposed to laugh at and knows all the taboos, but a child is a fresh slate.

The smile of pleasure appears after four days and laughter appears after six months. If you grab a baby's nose he will laugh unless he has developed a trauma from having his nose pinched too hard. The time-honored phrase "Bory-bory, boo!" will get satisfactory results, at least to the extent of causing the baby to express good humor at getting attention.

I would assume that a baby gets pretty lonely lying there like a dud for all those hours, and that getting attention would raise his spirits, which in one way or another is pretty close to the beginning of a sense of humor. My impression is that a healthy, jolly, laughing baby is seldom observed in a morose family, but that when the mother is of good spirits the baby gets the message that the world is a happy place.

Babies love the thrill of danger. It amuses them to be hung

39

out over a balcony, or to be held upside-down at the end of Daddy's long arm. "Daddy's got you," says Daddy, as he dangles baby over the edge of a fifty-foot cliff. If baby laughs he may be laughing at the dichotomy between great danger and great safety. It appears to strike him funny that he is going to be rescued from peril, and if so he is laughing at an opposite.

Having come across a statement of a generality in a book on the subject of humor, beginning "All children . . ." I hasten to assert that there is no such thing as "all children." There are grave children, utterly humorless children, and children with a great rascally sense of humor. It is a miniaturization of the adult world.

Humor begins in the family. Each family has its own sense of humor. If one does not come from a climate of humor one does not respond easily to comedy on the stage, does not like cartoons, hates amusing remarks, and is a plain grump.

A person with a really good sense of humor comes from a family with one. It may not be highly developed but the seed bed is there and it can be developed as one goes along. It is a way of life in some families that expresses itself in fun and games, and making light of troubles and of each other. These people have lots of fun in college and take insults easily.

Mark Twain fondly recalls dropping a watermelon rind on his brother's head from a second-story window. While Mark Twain seems to write better than I do, I consider myself his superior in dropping things out of windows.

In the normal give and take of life with my three brothers, one of my most satisfying experiences was to fill a brown paper bag with water from the cold-water faucet in the bathroom and drop it on the head of a brother passing by close to the house on the lawn below.

A Sense of Humor

A direct hit would not only distribute two quarts of water evenly over the whole body, but would also cause the bag to break into four equal flaps of brown paper which draped themselves tightly over the victim's head, rendering him unable to see where he was going. It was well to leave the bathroom at once and get settled in the living room, so that anyone seeking an audience would find you engrossed in a book.

Family humor is like national humor. Most people whose background is the British Isles have some kind of a sense of humor. They can laugh at themselves. Germans laugh at themselves less frequently and Russians hardly ever.

The acid test of a sense of humor is to have one about oneself. The over-important French alderman covered with ribbons who participates in some puffed-up event can ill afford to slip and fall into the canal. On the other hand Picasso put on clowns' noses or appeared in the bathtub wearing a funny hat without finding himself in jeopardy. Artists without Picasso's long view of life wear flowing capes and berets and are fond of making ponderous statements.

Different people react to the same piece of humor in different ways, like the child shown a picture of Christian martyrs being thrown to the lions, who said: "Look at the poor little lion away in the back. He's not going to get any."

If you ask two people who have laughed at a cartoon what they are laughing at you will get two different answers. It is like a discussion of beauty. Sophia Loren is beautiful to one person and not to another.

If you ask various people what they think of wealth the sour-grape people will assure you that no wealthy person is happy. If someone catches his toe in the carpet and falls flat on his face, one person will say, "It's a shame that happened to him. Especially on his anniversary." But someone who detests him and has been waiting all his life for something like this to happen will laugh uncontrollably.

The appreciation of humor roughly corresponds to the reader's character. Some people like jokes based on violence and antagonism. Others prefer English whimsey and understatement.

An impotent man, helpless in his position in life, may enjoy violence vicariously. Rosy Greer, weighing 400 pounds, sits there and does needlework, quite sure of himself and without fear. But a man who thinks his masculinity is in jeopardy might be attracted to violence, enjoy strong satire or jokes in which the weak person is the butt, because of his own weakness.

There is a lot of false dignity in the world. Some people feel that certain codes of conduct are forced upon them. Yet no one responds to humor more forthrightly than the sufferer from enforced dignity.

A doctor, for example, may feel that he must have a manner that evokes confidence. If such a doctor sees a satire on medicine—Al Kelly's wonderful straight-faced, double-talk address to a medical convention, for instance—no one will laugh harder than the doctor. Yet it would never do for the doctor to come into his waiting room full of dying people slapping his thighs.

Lots of dignified women would never think of acting in an amusing way, but will let the fat woman in the club do it for them, saying, "Oh, isn't she a scream?" Every group has such a scapegoat who permits them to go on being dignified and double-breasted and at the same time enjoy the laughter which restores their good spirits.

But in general all sophisticated people have some skill at

nonsense and satire. While doing the dishes on the maid's night out a couple may pretend to become two servants, discuss the man and woman of the house, criticize imaginary guests, and carry the impromptu playlet to great creative heights.

It is a more sophisticated version of children playing on a rainy afternoon. One allows one's brain to hang, away from the routine of life. Some people get paid for about the same thing. It is not a far carry from such a sketch form to the stage. It is a game played by some people with the object of seeing how ridiculous and extreme they can be.

The average layman cannot do this. People who come from a morose family, without any sense of humor of their own, are forced to get humor from the outside. To the degree that they lack a sense of humor they can be mechanically operated on by a formula. These are the people who say of the formula comedian, "At least he gives you a laugh." They say nothing about Charles Callas, do not respond to such original humor, and are frightened by it.

The Human Clod can agree only with something he already knows and cannot imagine something he does not already know. The sophisticated man is dying to be surprised, to comprehend, and to move on to something else. The Clod is constantly digging you in the ribs with his elbow to call your attention to something that struck him funny last year and the year before. Yet it does not take brains to have a sense of humor. Many intelligent men are as dry as bones. It all goes back to family and temperament.

Laughter and tears are brought on by the emotions. Every single human emotion is involved in tragedy and comedy. Comedy pulls different strings. One can make a child start laughing in the middle of a big bawling episode. No one has ever succeeded in making a squirrel laugh. I am not so sure about the dolphin.

I remember seeing a dolphin take a grouper gently by the tail and hold the grouper back from his lunch. Each time the grouper got close to his lunch the dolphin took the grouper's tail in his mouth, without injuring the grouper in the slightest, and held him back. Finally the dolphin allowed the grouper to go on to his lunch. I am afraid this is a sense of humor and I prefer not to get into it.

But on the whole humorists are lucky that people are members of the human race. If people were not human the humorist would have no springboard from which to get at them. There are no theaters for animals to go to, and there is no use getting out a humor magazine for them.

7

Rejection

The subconscious mind is fond of saying that he knows what he knows. In the middle of a conversation about peanuts one can laugh in rejection of the idea that peanuts grow under the ground, and not on peanut bushes as one had always thought, at the same time the intelligence accepts the statement as being true. This is called changing one's mind, and the subconscious mind will need a moment or so to change his peanut file.

The subconscious mind is always ready with a laugh at anything contrary to the information in his files. He laughed when Columbus said the world was round, and now laughs if anybody says it isn't. A man I know used to laugh at the extraordinary idea that the continents move, and now laughs if anybody says they don't. The noise that sent the tiger away has become the laughter of rejection.

Everything one has ever seen or heard is stored up by the subconscious mind in his files. He consults these files whenever a humorist enters the room. When he hears that a man arrested for smoking in bed has said to the judge, "Your Honor, that bed was on fire when I got into it," he examines his files carefully and the false logic is discovered.

One responds to humor with more or less laughter according to the way it affects one's state of satisfaction, without being aware of the cause of laughter. Things that sound right are accepted. Things that sound wrong are rejected. Any deviation from the agreed-on behavior of a culture is considered shocking. In addition our behavior is guided by a deep-seated drive to gain security and recognition and to avoid looking like a fool.

It is only the opposite or the exaggeration within the humor structure that the subconscious mind protects us from. It is not the ideas presented in humor that are rejected and laughed at. The ideas are almost always true, or at any rate what we believe to be true, and we agree with the ideas, accept them with pleasure and enjoy them. One no more laughs at truth than one laughs at beauty. The two are practically the same thing anyhow.

Truth brings pleasure because it is a relief to recognize it. It is a rare, almost extinct commodity, little spoken. Consciously or not most people are seeking after the truth. They hide from it, dodge it, and put their heads in the sand. But deep down they want to know the truth, the meaning of life and so on. There is something devastating and disarming about the truth. It has a purifying effect on people and puts them at their ease. One can trust someone who tells the truth.

The ordinary person is not able to think in the same terms used by the humorist, but the humorous remark with the ring of truth usually confirms what he had always suspected. Lots of people thought that Calvin Coolidge was a rather quiet man. When Dorothy Parker was told that Calvin Coolidge was dead, she said, "How can they tell?" which is merely a humorist's exaggeration of a basically true thing. The reader's slow to surface opinion said: "Right! That's right! Exactly!"

Coolidge himself was capable of using a basic truth as a starting point: "What this country wants as a president is a solemn ass, and I intend to give them one."

Will Rogers, making use of the basic truth that nobody can remember names, when introduced to Coolidge, leaned forward and said, "I didn't catch the name."

We accept with pleasure the idea in Oliver Wendell Holmes's paradox and agree with the truth it expresses. It is only the transposed position of the words we reject and laugh at. We agree with the truth in Voltaire's ideas in Micromegas and reject only the exaggeration of a man 120,000 feet tall with a nose 6,333 feet long. We accept the truth that catfish grow to be very large and laugh only at the exaggeration that catfish grow to be 18 feet long.

We reject with laughter too much effort to accomplish little or too little effort to accomplish much. We reject a too-large anything or a too-small anything. We laugh at too much bodily motion or too little, and regard the exaggeration of facial expressions as funny when they are more extreme than are necessary to suit the occasion, as in the extremes of crying or surprise shown us by Jerry Lewis. But we do not laugh at or reject the reason he is crying or the thing he is surprised by. We laugh only at an opposite or an extreme. Mental stability demands their rejection.

Our reaction to the opposite in a pun in defense of our mental comfort can be compared to brushing away a fly in defense of our physical comfort. I can account for the laughter at humor in no other way but by assuming that our concern for the slightest disturbance of our mental state as represented by our judgment and knowledge goes far beyond anything one might ordinarily suppose.

Our subconscious defense not only repels a serious attack on a deep-seated belief, which can be compared to a physical attack that might result in serious wounds. It not only entails a total resistance to the incorrect positions of syllables and words in such things as paradoxes and metatheses. I am of the opinion that the protection of our self-esteem and mental comfort, insofar as the attacks of the opposites and exaggerations of humor are concerned, parallels in the most minute detail our concern for physical comfort as expressed in such minor matters as moistening our lips, scratching an itch, or rejecting a lumpy mattress.

I can think of nothing else that would at once explain our exactly similar reaction—that of laughter—to a pun, an imitation of Streisand, a practical joke, the satire of Voltaire, and a man slipping on a banana peel, except the fact that each of them has buried within it an opposite or an exaggeration which the subconscious mind rejects with his old tiger noise.

If a golfer hits a ball into a cornfield the subconscious mind becomes suspicious. It is an opposite. It is the wrong place to hit a golf ball. The subconscious mind suspects that it is an attempt to make him think that it is the right place to hit a golf ball. If the golfer hits the next six balls in a row into the cornfield he becomes certain of it. The exaggeration reinforces the attempt to make him think that a cornfield is the proper place to hit a golf ball and he rejects the idea with laughter.

That the attack on his belief is not intentional makes no difference to the subconscious mind. If a brick falls on one's foot the pain is the same whether the brick was dropped deliberately or fell accidentally. There is a tiger present and the reason for its presence is not important. A headline that reads "Large crows at Methodist Church" is funny whether the typesetter left out the "d" in "crowds" by accident or on purpose.

48

Rejection

Certain motions are not accepted by society or by the individual. One learns to walk as a child and is told that the toes should point slightly outward. If the toes point too far outward one is said to walk like a duck. It is an exaggeration. If the toes point inward one is said to be pigeon-toed. It is an opposite.

All motions and positions of the body which exceed the margins allowed by society are forbidden. To take steps that are too long, say a yard and a half, or steps that are too short, say four inches, is considered funny. The subconscious mind rejects such motions and considers them to be an attack. He interprets them as an attempt to make him think it is the correct way to walk.

Swinging the arms wildly, walking in a crouch, and various gyrations while walking are also rejected by the subconscious mind who, while not overly shrewd in some areas, is an expert when it comes to recognizing an attack.

When a man slips on a banana peel and falls flat on his back on the sidewalk it is considered funny. The subconscious mind rejects this attempt to make him think that the proper way to walk along the sidewalk includes falling down.

There is a tiger present. There is no use pointing at the banana peel and telling him that if it were not for the banana peel the tiger would not be here. He has not the slightest interest in the reason for the tiger's appearance.

Whether the tiger is here because of the banana peel, or because the tiger is thirsty and there is a water hole just beyond the next hill, makes no difference whatever. The reason for the tiger's appearance is of no importance. The fact that the tiger has appeared is the only thing that interests the subconscious mind. It must be repelled. He is going to make his noise that frightens tigers away and nothing can stop him.

It has been noted that if a man who slips and falls on a

banana peel is badly injured, laughter stops immediately. This has been put down to commiseration, but I think that commiseration has nothing whatever to do with it. Laughter stops because his position is no longer incorrect. A man flat on his back on the sidewalk is in the correct position for an injured person. Since his position is correct there is no longer an attack on the observer's judgment.

The laughter and the stopping of laughter are rapid and unconscious reactions to the observer's knowledge of correct and incorrect positions on sidewalks. Commiseration is a conscious concern and may or may not be present. If it is present it does not prevent a visual image of your appearance while falling from creeping back into the observer's mind, thus renewing the attack on the observer's sense of rightness.

As he helps you to your feet you may notice going on in the observer a violent attempt to control his features, which is only moderately successful. This process may continue on and off all day and you might as well get used to it.

Familiarity and recognition are linked to the judgment and knowledge that one defends. One knows certain things and has certain skills. The humorist must find an area of self-regard, for it is in these areas that the reader may be attacked. If one is not familiar with a subject or if a skill is lacking it is of no consequence.

Confronted with evidence that one has burned a potato one shrugs. One is not a cook. If one fails to understand the point of a cartoon showing a woman pushing a baby carriage with a large letter "L" on the front of the carriage, one is not disturbed. Self-justification is not involved because none of one's friends would understand it either. In England, everyone understands that it announces a learner-driver.

Some cartoonists go through the morning newspaper while drinking their orange juice, clipping out items which have an element of familiarity to the general public. The familiarity may consist of some facet of a continuing subject, such as crime, or a story revealing a familiar human emotion, such as frustration, and perhaps giving a detailed account of a man who emptied a forty-five revolver into the screen of his television set.

The cartoonist may put a crown on any character he chooses and the reader will at once say to himself, "Ah! A king!" If he puts a crown on a rabbit, the reader will say, "Ah. The king of the rabbits." This is recognition and the immediate acceptance and understanding of a common idea. The cliché, by its nature, is understood and accepted by the reader. He needs no explanation of a cliché character such as the scientist with his laboratory coat, beard, and eyeglasses, or of a cliché setting such as a convict's cell or a desert island.

Man is a thinking animal. A lifetime of experience is stored in the billions of molecules in his nerve cells. He can draw upon them at will. Sometimes he draws upon them and nothing comes out. He is not familiar with the subject. For this reason most humor is based on topical things or universal things. One's judgment is guided by what one can recollect of a subject.

Topicality compliments one on one's knowledge. The assumption that the reader is alert to what is happening and abreast of the news is complimentary. A joke based on Einstein's Theory of Relativity, told to a scientist, is complimentary in the same way. The mere fact that he is told the joke assumes knowledge on his part.

Things go out of fashion. Every dog has his day. One cannot make jokes about World War II rationing forever. There is a new viewpoint on food. The clergyman-parishioner relationship is reversed. Respect is gone and there are gimmicks on the bulletin boards to get the congregation in. The clergyman has become a lackey figure lucky to have anybody in the congregation.

The relationship of the educator to the student is another complete reversal as a source of humor. The white-haired professor no longer exists. The professor is now a thirty-five-year-old seedy bum, and the student body looks like the contents of a derelict ship who have fallen victim to a plague.

Old maids who used to be laughed at are now glorified and called Ms. It is married women who are laughed at and the housewife is apologetic about her status. Cops continue as a source of humor but not because they steal apples. Daumier showed a parent slapping a child. Today the child quotes psychiatric jargon to the parent.

Doctors are always a good butt for jokes because they are so prestigious that if they make mistakes it is pretty funny, as in the case of the doctor who signed his name in the space reserved for "cause of death." In the servant-master relationship the servant is no longer trembling beneath the stairs but is guaranteed a color television set and is taken from door to door in a limousine.

Comments on sexual mores go on from decade to decade, and humor is composed out of whatever is current. Living together before marriage was never discussed in the 1940s because it was not there to be discussed. But now that one is free to do anything it has become material for salable humor, and Frank Modell has one of his New Yorker cartoon characters say, "Your father and I never did anything funny before we were married."

The universal things are always familiar, and what Daumier had to say about judges still applies. The male-female situations are eternal, and Thurber's work is as good as it ever was.

8

Convincingness

An opposite is the basis of all humor, and convincingness is the thing that makes the opposite work. Without an opposite there is no humor. Without convincingness there is no humor. Together they form the humor structure.

In caricature one may lengthen the nose. The exaggeration of the length of the nose is an opposite. The likeness of the person is convincingness. In a pun the similarity of the word is convincingness, the fact that it is a nonword is an opposite. In a paradox the construction of the sentence is convincingness, the transposed positions of the words is an opposite.

Anything that strikes the reader as being correct adds to the sum total of convincingness. The use of this word instead of that, the form of a sentence, including punctuation, the description of character, even so briefly as "a farmer," or "an old farmer," or "a farmhand," the description of setting, even so short a description as "on a boat," or "on a ship," or "on a yacht," all add to or detract from convincingness.

The subconscious mind always reasons: "If this is right and that is right and this is right, then that is right, too." But it is

53

not. It is an opposite which has been presented with a greater or lesser degree of convincingness and is rejected with a greater or lesser degree of laughter.

The manner of telling—that is, the style—is a part of convincingness. The degree of the reader's familiarity with the subject and its relative importance to his ego are factors in the success of the attack by the opposite. But how much laughter is evoked by a piece of humor depends mainly on the oppositeness of the opposite, and the convincingness of the convincingness. The more of each the better, provided they balance each other.

This is the humor structure. It requires balance. One teeters along. An outrageous opposite requires strong convincingness. A strong opposite with weak convincingness is not laughed at. One is not convinced that anything has happened, in spite of being plainly told that it has, and the subconscious mind reasons that if nothing has happened there is nothing to laugh at.

A weak opposite with strong convincingness is not laughed at either. The reader is convinced that what you say is true, therefore he has not been attacked. If he has not been attacked there is no reason to defend himself by making his tiger noise.

What is needed is balance, false logic presented so convincingly that it takes a moment to discover, but not so convincingly that it cannot be discovered. The reader laughs as soon as he is attacked and feels pleasure as soon as he discovers the false logic. It should take him about 5/6 of a second to find it and during that time he is horrified.

Because I more or less know what I was trying to do when I wrote the following piece, I will use it as an example of the way one teeters along, applying convincingness wherever it is needed to shore up oppositeness.

54

Convincingness

TEST*

Rate Yourself in Savoir Faire

1. Your host for the evening is a world-famous violinist. After the coffee has been served, he is prevailed upon to play a small but charming sonatina by Schubert. At the final note, the E string snaps and opens a cruel gash in his forehead. He hands his eighteenth-century Guarnerius to you and asks you to take care of it while he finds a bandage. As you are leaning over to examine the sap marks, your cigarette falls through one of the sound holes into the interior of the violin. Shaking the violin upside down does no good.

You should:

(a) Hand the violin to one of the other guests.

(b) Pry open the back of the violin just far enough to allow the cigarette to fall out.

(c) Dip the violin in a bucket of water.

2. You are one of a large party of weekend guests at a château near Paris. The bedroom assigned to you by your host gives off the top gallery and is entered through the seventh door on the left, counting from the top of the alternate stairway. The top floor of the château has no illumination of any kind, and you are forced to prepare for bed in the dark. As you lie in bed musing over the activities of the day, you become aware that there is someone else in the bed.

You should:

(a) Find out if it is a man or a woman.

(b) Try to imitate a snoring poodle.

(c) Go to sleep.

*© 1970 The New Yorker Magazine, Inc.

55

3. As president of the renowned Quintly Ironworks, you are host at a brilliant dinner party held in the executive dining room of the main factory. The governor of the state is a guest, and after cigars and liqueurs he expresses a desire to tour the plant. He shows a keen interest in the two-hundred-ton crane, the hundred-foot-high blast furnaces, and the twenty-thousand-ton hydraulic forging press. He is examining the taphole in the bottom of one of the huge ingot-molding buckets when you accidentally lean against a lever that releases twenty tons of molten steel into the bucket.

You should:

(a) Poke around in the bucket with a ladle to see if you can find the governor.

(b) Change the labelling on the ingot to read "20 tons, 175 lbs."

(c) Run for governor.

4. You have come down from your chalet in Switzerland to the Argentario for dinner with the Cecil Aberfords at their *pied-à-terre* in Port'Ercole. While awaiting the dinner gong, you examine a fine *marmo di Castellina* statuette representing Persephone discarding a pomegranate core. The head of the statuette comes off in your hands.

You should:

(a) Go back up to your chalet.

(b) Ask your hostess for a jar of Elmer's Glue-All.

(c) Put the head in your pocket and go in to dinner.

5. As a member of our diplomatic corps, you have gone to Budapest to meet with Count Zsigmond von Esterházy in an effort to improve our relations with his gov-

ernment. His villa atop Sváb-Hegy is reached by a quaint rack-and-pinion railway. On the way up the beetling mountainside, the Count is at the controls of the engine; back in the open observation car, you are holding the Countess up so she can see Zugló when suddenly you sneeze and drop her.

You should:

(a) Find a Kleenex in your luggage.

(b) Ask the Count if the Countess is up there with him.

(c) Wire Washington for instructions.

6. Before a holiday tour of the Continent, you are spending a few days in the London home of Huang Chow, an expatriated member of the oldest dynastic family of China. One night during your stay, there is a sudden ice storm, and you make yourself useful by finding several containers of ashes in the basement and scattering them on the slippery driveway and front steps of the house. The following morning, you discover that they were the ashes of several of Huang Chow's ancestors.

You should:

(a) Continue on to the Continent.

(b) Look outdoors to see if there has been a thaw.

(c) Offer to replace the ashes with some others just as good.

7. Against your surgeon's wishes, you are attending the Poetry Awards Dinner at the White House to receive the Gold Medal for your poem "A Lock of Mother's Hair." The minor awards have already been given out and it is about time for you to go forward when your appendix bursts.

You should:

(a) Ask the President to bring the medal to your table.

(b) Go forward in a low crouch.

(c) Add a joking reference to Medicare in your acceptance speech.

8. While driving to California, you stop off in Nevada to visit your sister, who has just married a career officer in the Army. She tells you to make yourself at home while she goes to fetch him at the base. There are three refrigerators in the apartment, and you find beer in one of them, a piece of blue cheese in another, and some moldy crackers in the third. You have just finished off your repast when she returns and introduces you to her husband. It turns out that he is a bacteriologist doing plague research for the government.

You should:

(a) Ask him what type plagues he is working on at present.

(b) Turn the conversation to cheeses.

(c) Look around in an offhand way for a clinical thermometer.

9. In your capacity as curator of forgeries at the Metropolitan Museum, you are one of a group of art experts visiting the Italian galleries. The group is invited by Count Umbroglio di Bombolino to spend a few days at his palazzo in Venice. One evening, the Count remarks that he has reason to believe that the painting in your bedroom—"Bringing in the Cows," by Guglielmo Gigli —has been painted over a profile view of the Mona Lisa. That night, before going to bed, you take a can of benzine and begin the delicate operation of removing the

upper layer of paint. When you have finished soaking the canvas, you scrape it carefully with a razor blade. Both paintings come off, leaving you with a handful of pigment chips.

You should:

(a) Feign madness.

(b) Lower yourself into the Grand Canal and swim to a hotel.

(c) Glue the paint back on the canvas in an amusing pointillist style.

10. At last a child has been born to your old friends the Duke and Duchess of Ravensthorpe, who are both in their forties. You accompany the Duke to the local nursing home. Left alone in the nursery, you observe that someone, probably a novice interne, has tied a string onto a toe of all six babies in the room. Fearing that the tight strings will interfere with the circulation in their little toes, you remove the strings. Then you notice that a tiny identification tag is attached to each string.

You should:

(a) Check to see if any of the babies has lank blond hair and prominent front teeth.

(b) Eliminate any babies with strong chins.

(c) Tie the Ravensthorpe identification tag on the best baby.

Ratings:

(The correct answer *in each case* is "c.")

10-8 correct: Excellent. You have ambience, cachet, and the ability to think rapidly in almost any social situation. You know when to bring out your solid-gold tea service, when the wine steward is lying, and who precedes whom into the sauna. Sixty-five per cent of those scoring 8 or more have no difficulty in correctly introducing three archbishops to each other, and can recognize new money at a distance of forty feet.

7-3 correct: Quite good, really. You must fight against a tendency to stay overnight without being invited. You are ready for small dinners, or any functions held by your union. A score of less than 5 reveals a mild feebleness of intellect, and repartee should not be attempted without written notes. Whenever possible, stay in large groups.

2-0 correct: Poor to miserable. Try to cut down on lapel-grasping and chest-poking with the forefinger. You are weak on leave-taking and, in general, should leave shortly after you arrive. You can safely accept any invitations written on brown wrapping paper. You are a good listener, and you should push that.

The form of the test is familiar to the reader and is acceptable. He has seen other tests and recognizes the form as correct and therefore convincing. The use of (a), (b), and (c) is also acceptable. The reader is accustomed to seeing possible answers presented as three choices labeled (a), (b), and (c).

Of the three choices he knows that two will be wrong, and he is not alarmed when he deems (a) to be incorrect. It does nothing to destroy convincingness. In such tests two of three choices are always wrong. But when (b) and (c) are both deemed incorrect by the reader, question 1 becomes an opposite. There has been an attempt to fool the reader.

In question 2 the problem is to get someone to prepare for

bed in a pitch-black room without turning on the light, and then without knowing it to get into bed with a stranger. Without solving this problem of convincingness one cannot arrive at any humor in the choice of answers offered in (a), (b), and (c), one of which I find very funny, and, indeed, fell off my chair while writing it. The attempt to convince the reader that the situation is plausible goes as follows:

1. There are large weekend parties.
2. A bedroom would be assigned.
3. An old French château would be a large rambling labyrinth with odd turns and twists, different stairways, and confusing corridors. One might easily lose one's way and get into the wrong bedroom.
4. One has read that parts of such great houses are unoccupied and can accept the idea that there is no electricity on the top floor.

Without this supporting convincingness the subconscious mind would not consider himself to have been attacked, for the same reason that a pun in which the imitative word has no close resemblance to the real word is not laughed at. If one is told as a part of a joke that a man walked on the ceiling, and something like glue on the bottom of his shoes is not mentioned, it is an opposite that is not laughed at because there is no convincingness present. It is simply disbelieved.

If the ceiling is sheet iron and the man is wearing magnetized boots there is no laughter because convincingness is complete. There has been no attempt to fool the hearer. There has been no attack, nothing to reject. The hearer fully accepts the idea that the man could walk on the ceiling.

In question 3 the problem is to convince the reader that the governor is in the bottom of a bucket. In order to have a dinner in the main dining room of a factory with a governor in attendance one needs an invitation from the president of the company to the governor.

Once the governor is inside the ironworks the reader easily accepts the idea that he is shown around. Anyone of any consequence who visits a plant of any sort is shown around. Things are going easily and the reader is accepting everything. For this reason he is inclined to accept the unfortunate leaning against the lever.

Having accepted the situation the first choice offered the reader as to what to do is so completely opposed to the reader's judgment that it is rejected with laughter at once, especially as it contains within itself rather strong convincingness. Poking around in murky liquid looking for something is so familiar to the reader and so correct a thing to do that the exaggeration of poking around for a governor becomes a violent attack.

Question 4. The purpose of the details leading to the breaking of the statuette is to establish the costliness of the thing broken. The more expensive and irreplaceable it is the stronger the opposite.

The convincingness consists largely of the reader's familiarity with things coming apart in the hands. The presence of the statuette is accepted because people like the Aberfords might well own a statuette of this kind. An excuse for the culprit being in the room is given—an invitation to dinner. An excuse for his standing around is given—dinner is not ready. The reader himself supplies further convincingness simply by knowing that in such a situation people wander around and inspect things.

Question 5. The reader would not accept the idea of dropping a countess off a mountainside without some explanation.

Convincingness

The incident must be made plausible. The reader's subconscious mind reasons that a member of the American diplomatic corps might go to Hungary and might meet a countess. The name von Esterházy is accepted as Hungarian, and the reader has heard about those funny railways. Having accepted the railway, the reader has allowed the countess to get up on the side of a mountain. It remains only to drop her.

Question 6. Ashes are ashes. Once the situation is explained the reader quite accepts the idea that someone might mistakenly spread them on ice.

Question 7. The greatest problem was the difficulty of convincing the reader that anyone with advanced appendicitis would attend a public dinner. The fact that he is going to receive a gold medal helps and would save most of the humor. But after finishing this one I put at the beginning the words "Against your surgeon's wishes. . . ."

The fact that people constantly disregard their doctor's orders added convincingness. The difficulty remained that a surgeon's orders sound more important than a doctor's orders, and might raise in the reader's mind some slight doubt that the poet did in fact appear at the dinner. The fact that I said he did makes no difference to the subconscious mind. He must be convinced of it. For this reason I used the word "wishes" instead of "orders." The reader accepts the fact that wishes are more easily disregarded than orders.

Convincingness is only one part of humor but it is an essential part. Basically the degree of convincingness lost matches exactly the degree of humor lost. The more convincing an imitation of another person the funnier it is. The more convincing a nonword is the funnier the pun is. The more convincingly the opposite is presented in a joke the more violent is the laughter with which it is rejected.

Question 8. The whole preamble is devoted to convincing the reader that there are three refrigerators in an apartment and that poison is kept in them.

Question 9. In this one I have managed to get an incompetent art expert (curator of forgeries) into a small room by himself in company with a valuable painting. Until the reader can be convinced that this situation exists there can be very little humor.

From then on one walks a tightrope of convincingness. The reader can understand the guest wanting to repay the host for his kindness. Benzine sounds almost right as a material to be used. Scraping the canvas with a razor blade gains some acceptance because of the word "carefully," and because the reader knows that lots of things can be cleaned by scraping them with a razor blade. None of this convincingness is completely dismissed by the reader until the whole thing falls apart.

Question 10. The reader must be convinced that someone would remove identification tags from the toes of newborn babies. Fear that tight strings might interfere with the circulation in their little toes is completely acceptable to all females, especially if the dumbbell doing it is a male. We can then get on with (a), (b), and (c), none of them acceptable to anyone.

For the sake of strengthening the opposite, the importance of the object is stressed (in this case a baby) by saying "at last," and by giving the mother's age. For the same reason the statuette was valuable, the person dropped from a mountainside was a countess, the painting was a Mona Lisa, the violin was a Guarnerius, and the person in the bottom of a bucket was a governor.

The form of the answers to the questions is acceptable to

the reader down to the smallest detail of the ratings system. He has seen it all before and accepts its rightness. However, the string of insults consists of a series of opposites, opposite to what he has come to expect in such tests.

To aid convincingness as many modifying words as possible are sprinkled among the insults, in themselves opposites to be fended off, such as "Quite good, really," or "You are ready" for this or that function, or that one's feebleness of mind is "mild." But the reader detects the opposites with their false logic everywhere and rejects the whole thing.

In all humor something is presented which is not accepted by the reader. It may be a misspelling, or words out of position, or an emphasis out of position, or a motion of the body which has been exaggerated. Whatever it is, the humorist, having arrived at the opposite he is going to use, bends all his effort toward convincing the reader of its correctness.

One uses false logic. A haystack is enough to break a fall from an airplane. Steel springs on the feet will enable one to jump to the second story of a building. Fortunately one need fool only the subconscious mind, who dropped out of school fifteen million years ago, whose files are in some disorder, whose associative paths have breaks in them, and whose visual images include many light-struck photographs.

9

Puns

The making of a pun is a dear little trick of seeing two things that resemble each other and putting them together. One is the thing, the other is the nonthing. Thus the two things that resemble each other constitute an opposite. The fact that they are like each other also provides the convincingness.

Punning has got a bad name because it is not often in the right hands. But sometimes it is. This pun is from an opera synopsis by Robert Benchley:

> Lucy is seen surrounded by every luxury, but her heart is sad. She has just been shown a forged letter from Stewart saying that he no longer loves her, and she remembers her old free life in the mountains and longs for another romp with Ravensbane and Wolfshead, her old pair of rompers.

Puns are disliked for the same reason that practical jokes are disliked. The joke is on the person to whom it is told. He

66

has fallen for something. There is a slight double-cross involved. However, there are certain people who don't mind getting a hotfoot, so long as they are permitted to keep on giving hotfoots.

Most puns are thick ankled. The punster's conversation is full of women who do not care for overwrought iron, doctors who send bills with a note saying, "Long time no fee," and Indians who remark that they are all just one big Hopi family.

There are those who can't or won't make puns. They haven't the kind of nimbleness of mind that enables one to pull needles out of two different haystacks, and they show their disapproval of puns by groaning. The truth is that the punster has a very lively mind, and there is no such thing as a really dumb pun. Either they come across or they don't.

Max Beerbohm, declining an invitation to accompany a group of mountain-climbers, said: "Put me down as an anticlimb Max."

When Syngman Rhee was working for *Life* magazine, someone spotted him on Fifth Avenue and said: "Ah, sweet Mr. Rhee of *Life*, at last I've found you."

The pun maker is careful to present the pun in such a way that it cannot be mistaken for a solecism. He usually leans heavily on the fact that he is brilliant and well educated. The construction of a pun makes him feel creative with the language, slightly superior, and the possessor of a cultivated mind because he is seen to be at home with a great many references to the theater, literature, and art.

Samuel Johnson was proud of being able to make a pun instantly on any subject. When someone suggested the king, Johnson replied, "My dear sir, the king is not a subject." Other puns are somewhat more laboriously prepared:

Charlie Chan collected teakwood and kept it in a pile in his back yard. One night it was stolen. Charlie found boys' footprints in the yard and followed them to a cave in the woods. He entered the cave and found his teakwood, as well as a bear which instead of having paws had boys' feet. In other words, a boy-foot bear with teak of Chan.

When someone adopts a voice like an old woman and pretends to be Truman Capote, or hunches up his shoulders and imitates his friend George, he is making a pun. It shares the same structure as a pun in which a word imitates another word. Both are opposites in the sense that one is the non-George and the other the nonword.

The laughter they produce involves rejection of them by the audience. They know what George looks like and how he speaks. They see that the imitator looks and sounds like George, and they laugh in self-justification to announce that they know he is not George, that they see the resemblance, that they get the point.

If one merely looks and sounds like George the laughter need be merely enough to make them feel adequate again. To construct a better piece of humor something else will have to be added. Thus one exaggerates George's manner of walking or of wearing his hat, or carries to an extreme his mannerisms of speaking.

A word that imitates another word and an imitation of George are laughed at for the same reasons. The audience will laugh at the sentence "To purify the city's water it is forced through an aviator," to announce that the proper word is known to them. If they remained silent those around them might suppose that the proper word was unknown to them.

This habit of rejection and self-justification is so strong that people will laugh for the same reasons even when alone.

The value of exaggeration in a visual pun is illustrated in the following practical joke in which an imitation of feet is the basic pun. The exaggeration is carried as far as any belief can be expected and the whole structure of the joke is made into a clever attack upon the observer's judgment and knowledge, and carries with it a precise degree of convincingness together with a built-in escape:

> On a rainy day the professor left his rubbers in the cloakroom. Using flesh-color oil paint, which is impervious to water, some of his students painted large bare feet on the rubbers. They covered the painted feet with lamp-black water color, which would wash off in the rain. When this happened, the professor would be walking along the sidewalk in extremely large bare feet.

The basic opposite could be developed in a number of ways. One could paint all the convolutions of a brain on a black derby, or the bones of the hand on black gloves, or the entire nervous system on the back of a black raincoat. If one is sore at having missed the boat by painting realistically when abstract expressionism came in, one could release one's repressed aggression by using cadmium red, yellow ochre, white, a little olive green, and raw umber, to paint an opaque head on one of those transparent umbrellas. Humor somewhat depends on one's style.

10

Play With Words

Words are commonly used as a subject for humor because their use ensures a large audience. When the misuse of words is based on an opposite accompanied by convincingness, we defend our knowledge of correct speech behavior by laughing at such foolishnesses as:

My baby is about to have a wife.

A twenty-one sun galoot.

The Brown Quince of Denmark.

An uninhibited part of the earth.

A lot of things you are supposed to eat you just don't like—especially children.

I read Lewis Carroll's *Through the Looking-Glass* at a very early age under the impression that it was a children's book. When I came to things like Alice's exchange with the White King:

"I see nobody on the road," said Alice.

"I only wish *I* had such eyes," the King remarked in a

fretful tone. "To be able to see Nobody! And at that distance, too!"

I was astounded and delighted to learn that one was allowed to do that with words. I had been taught to spell correctly, to find out the meanings of words, and to place the predicate to the right-hand side of the subject. Our use of language is limited by a rigid code. When the code is broken there is often an attempt to fool us, as in this verse by Oliver Herford:

> My sense of sight is very keen
> My sense of hearing weak.
> One time I saw a mountain pass,
> But could not hear its peak.

There is a difference between play with words which is intended to fool the reader and play with words which simply brings pleasure. When the poet uses a metaphor to speak of a woman's "marble brow," he is not trying to make us think that the woman's forehead is solid marble. There is no attempt to fool us. He knows that we will understand that he means the woman's forehead is white, but he is so overcome with emotion that he cannot bring himself merely to say "white."

Such metaphors appeared fifteen million years ago and were the beginning of play with words. Words which stand for action and ideas come from roots having to do with the physical senses. The words "sun," "sea," and "dawn," all come from a root meaning "bright." The root for "comprehend" meant to grasp physically. From a root meaning "to strike" come the words for "ax" and "fist."

Aphorisms, allusions, and analogies are not meant to be

funny. In an allusion something is missing which must be supplied by the reader. But there is no attempt to fool the reader. On the contrary, an allusion is usually a compliment. There is a complimentary assumption that the reader will understand the allusion, to say nothing of the assumption that he can read.

In an analogy there is something to get, something to be transposed. But the transposition is easy, and the reader responds to an apt analogy with a smile of pleasure.

Nonsense, on the other hand, sets out to fool the reader. There is an attempt to slip something past his guard. Nonsense depends on an opposite or an exaggeration and must be accompanied by convincingness. A nonsense word is a nonword imitating a real word. To be successful it must carry some degree of convincingness either in sound association or in its relationship to other words in the sentence.

Lewis Carroll's "Jabberwocky" is seen at a glance to be a poem, which is reassuring, and it begins with " 'Twas." Lots of poems begin with " 'Twas," and the subconscious mind begins to feel that everything will be all right.

The second word is the neologism "brillig." The word is not immediately familiar to the reader, although he is pretty sure he has seen it someplace. He sees in "brillig" the first half of "brilliant," and deduces that since " 'Twas" something, 'Twas probably fairly brilliant. Moonlight, perhaps.

The reader is accustomed to making these lightning-like deductions, using his knowledge that any word beginning with "phil" probably means love of something, for example, or, if the word "neologism" is unfamiliar to him, deducing that if "brillig" is a neologism, "neologism" must mean "made-up word."

Humpty Dumpty's statement: "When I use a word it means

just what I choose it to mean—neither more nor less," was a revelation to me. Since reading it I have not hesitated to invent a word when the dictionary did not contain one with the exact meaning I wanted, or to maintain the correctness of my grammar, even when shown proof to the contrary. I once began a piece with this paragraph:

> I was somewhat surprised, recently, to receive a visit from my old friend, the well-known African explorer, Sir Bartroak Thrustrum. I had thought he had long since been chewn to death by a mongoose . . .

The word "chewn" is not to be found in any dictionary but is nevertheless quite understandable and I felt that its delicacy would be less objectionable than the word "chewed" to sensitive readers, since it suggested that the animal was taking quite small bites.

In his use of neologisms Lewis Carroll was careful to distribute clues either in the words or in the syntax so that the reader always receives a very clear picture of something, even if he is never quite sure what it is.

The music of Johann Strauss is for plain enjoyment, whereas listening to Mozart takes a lot out of you. One hears a great deal about the release of inhibitions in connection with humor, but I think that an amusing flight of fancy does not necessarily release any inhibitions. Neither does "having fun" with words by an intellectual, such tomfoolery with an intellectual content being similar to Lewis Carroll's work.

On the other hand a convention delegate, who is in private life a pompous dignified fool, gets drunk and uses those buzzers on the street and sure enough his inhibitions are released. He thinks he is "having fun," but the same thing would be a dull thud to an intellectual. A dignified man whose code of behavior does not permit him to be seen in his bathrobe needs a powerful release from his inhibitions.

The child who can talk nonsense successfully is a superior child. His nonsense is a primitive form of humor which in an adult becomes wit, and is the father of Lewis Carroll's nonsense. The child who flaps his tongue against his lips and produces "Blblb-bllb-blbbleddebblb!" or speaks gibberish is exploring and throwing things together that make him laugh.

11

Humorous Verse

There is a basic difference between light verse and humorous verse. Light verse is pleasant, humorous verse is funny. There are two kinds of humorous verse. The first attempts to fool the reader by presenting an opposite, a humor structure, in rhyme:

> As I was laying on the green
> A small English book I seen.
> Carlyle's *Essay on Burns* was the edition,
> So I left it laying in the same position.
> —*Anonymous*

The second kind of humorous verse has no basic humor structure. Instead there is an attempt to make the reader talk funny by using a carefully composed mixture of alliteration, cadence, rhyme, meter, and as many syllables as possible. All this contributes to an "incorrect" way of talking which can be made just as funny to the subconscious mind as an "incorrect" way of walking.

In reading the verse the reader is forced to speak in a manner far removed from his normal way of speaking, and to say foolish things that would not normally enter his conversation. The number of syllables per inch is increased to as many as possible, causing the reader to flap his tongue around at a high rate of speed, to adjust the opening of his glottis and the position of his palate with unaccustomed quickness, and to open and close his mouth as rapidly as possible.

Thus he already resembles a man working on an assembly line that has been speeded up so that it is all he can do to tighten each nut as it comes along. The writer then adds alliteration, inserting as many matching hard consonants as he can think of (vowels are no good), so that the reader is saying something like "Buh buh, tuh puh tuh," as in this line by Charles Carryl: ". . . the Binnacle-bats wore water-proof hats . . ."

All of this is far more important than the subject matter, or what is said about the subject matter. Therefore the subject matter is bent in whatever direction will increase the contrast between the way the reader ordinarily talks and the way he talks as he reads the verse.

There is always a limited supply of words containing the hard consonants one wants, which will at the same time lend themselves nicely to the meter and rhyme. If one wants two hard c's in a row one settles happily for "cabbages and kings." The fact that the reader has no time to stop and search for the connection between cabbages and kings, if there is any, merely increases the suspicions of the subconscious mind that this is not the right way to talk. It is part of an attack against which the subconscious mind will defend the self by laughing.

Edward Lear is quite happy with his percussions "k" and "t" and pleased to follow wherever they lead him:

Humorous Verse

O my aged Uncle Arly!
Sitting on a heap of barley
    Through the silent hours of the night—
Close beside a leafy thicket:
On his nose there was a cricket,
In his hat a Railway-Ticket;
    (But his shoes were far too tight.)

Alliteration in verse has a long and honorable history, and Coleridge, in "The Ancient Mariner," could not resist saying:

The fair breeze blew, the white foam flew
The furrow followed free . . .

The amount of humor in alliteration by itself can hardly rise higher than "Peter Piper picked a peck of pickled peppers." Meter, rhyme, and foolish words must be added so that the reader is kept busy fending things off.

The value of an inordinate number of syllables is made clear in Lear's use of the words "formerly garnished," in his verse about the pobble who lost his toes while swimming across the Bristol Channel:

. . . And when he came to observe his feet,
Formerly garnished with toes so neat . . .

After the important matters of alliteration, number of syllables, cadence, meter, and rhyme are settled, any choice that is left as to which foolish words to use depends on their intrinsic value as a further attack on the harried reader. Words which have even the slightest chance of being accepted by the subconscious mind are preferred, and are set up in a sentence

77

that is formed correctly so that the whole thing will be as convincing as possible.

The visual images are guided by the words that turn up. It hardly matters what they are, or what meaning they carry, just so they rhyme or have the proper alliteration, and fit the meter. If one has already used "thicket" and "cricket," there is not much left besides "ticket."

If the subject of a verse is pie, the subconscious mind reasons that glue is very much like pie filling in consistency, and that sawdust bears some vague resemblance to flour. So the slight convincingness carried by the phrase "sawdust and glue" causes the subconscious mind to hesitate.

Anything that strikes the subconscious mind as correct adds convincingness to the whole. Recipes are perfectly acceptable and Lewis Carroll gains convincingness by casting this verse from "The Hunting of the Snark" in the form of a recipe. "Jubjub" is a nonsense word, but when the word "bird" is added to it the subconscious mind frantically searches his file of African birds. Since nobody really knows how to cook a Jubjub bird Lewis Carroll hopes that the ingredients will look all right to the subconscious mind:

> You boil it in sawdust: you salt it in glue:
> You condense it with locusts and tape:
> Still keeping one principal object in view—
> To preserve its symmetrical shape.

There is a third kind of humorous verse which is simply a combination of the first two. One begins with a basic humor structure and crowds in as many of the other things as possible. Because of the limited number of words in the English language it is extremely difficult, except for Lewis Carroll, to get everything right.

If one has the alliteration one wants the rhyming word is not the precise word one needs for the joke. If the right word rhymes perfectly the alliteration is lost. If the alliteration and rhyming word are exactly right the meter is off. In one of my own verses, "Think of the Earth as a Shrunken Apple," I was forced to reduce the number of Saturn's rings to one:

> Just what is matter made of?
> How far away are stars?
> Is space as empty as they say?
> Are there canals on Mars?
>
> The answers to these questions
> Have never been made clear,
> Though books upon the subject
> Are published every year.
>
> The subject is a large one—
> Complexities are vast;
> But here, in simple terms, I have
> Explained it all at last.
>
> Think of space as made of soup
> And of the stars as noodles;
> Think that nebulae are cake,
> And moons are apple strudels.
>
> Imagine that the asteroids
> Are joined by bits of string;
> Imagine that a swarm of bees
> Accounts for Saturn's ring . . .*

---

*Reprinted with permission from *The Saturday Evening Post,* © 1950 by The Curtis Publishing Company.

Although I regretted eliminating several of Saturn's rings, I was determined to have that swarm of bees, and in order to get it I had to do the best I could with the rhyme.

For the same reason (small number of words in the English language) W. S. Gilbert resorts to an inversion. In "Gentle Alice Brown" the girl is confessing her sins to a priest, who asks: ". . . Whatever have you gone and done?"

I have helped mamma to steal a little kiddy from its dad;
I've assisted dear papa in cutting up a little lad;
I've planned a little burglary and forged a little cheque,
And slain a little baby for the coral on its neck!

The worthy pastor heaved a sigh, and dropped a silent tear—
And said, "You mustn't judge yourself too heavily, my dear—
It's wrong to murder babies, little corals for to fleece;
But sins like these one expiates at half-a-crown apiece."

Toward the end of the verse the English language ran out of suitable words, but Gilbert was determined to get the last line just as it stands and regretfully accepted the phrase, "little corals for to fleece," which gave him the rhyme but with the words out of their natural order.

In a verse from "The Hunting of the Snark," Lewis Carroll flawlessly accomplishes everything at once. A member of the crew has arrived to go on board for the voyage:

He had forty-two boxes, all carefully packed,
With his name painted clearly on each:
But, since he omitted to mention the fact,
They were all left behind on the beach.

The basic opposite is funny, the exaggeration of the num-

80

ber of boxes is funny, the order of words is completely natural, the beat of the meter is exact, the number of syllables is gratifyingly overwhelming, and the alliteration is frightening. If the hard consonants are arbitrarily rendered as buh, duh, and tuh, one arrives at something like this:

He had duh four-tuh-tuh buh, all carefully puh duh,
With his name muh puh tuh duh clearly on each:
Buh tuh, since he muh tuh duh tuh muh mention the fact tuh,
They were all left tuh buh behind duh on the buh beach.

I count four buhs, five duhs, and eight tuhs. It may be a record.

12

The Hidden Opposite

In the definition "effrontery is the other side of a behindery," the opposite is plain to see. But when the complication of an opposite is made complete with the addition of setting, character, and dialogue, the opposite sometimes becomes so veiled that it is difficult to discern.

Opposites need not necessarily spring to the eye. If they are there they do the same work as a perfectly bare, obvious opposite. One opposite may be added to another and the result spread through a long section of exaggeration and the whole veiled in some obscurity by dialogue and description, but if the right degree of convincingness trots along, the humor structures will lose none of their power.

An opposite may be overall. One might write a piece of humor in the form of a biography of a great financier who never made any money, or of a great artist who never painted anything. Swift uses an overall opposite in his satire in which he pretends that babies are the same thing as meat, to be sold over the counter.

Any opposite at all may be used as a basis for a piece of humor and will to some extent guide and affect any individual piece of humor the writer can think of. He has committed himself. If he has chosen a boy and a man as his two characters, and has decided on the overall opposite of making the boy more intelligent than the man, he must adhere to this opposite throughout the piece, and the dialogue between the two characters will be guided by it.

An incident involving an overall opposite occurred in my own childhood. The overall opposite consisted of behavior not acceptable to my social group, made convincing because of my tender age.

When I was six years old and in the first grade I lived in a small river town in Indiana. My route to school—which I had difficulty remembering—was left turn at the first corner, straight ahead for two blocks, and sharp right for two more blocks.

On one of my first journeys I had negotiated the left turn successfully and was trudging straight ahead when a woman called to me from her back porch and asked if I would like to stop in for some hot biscuits and jelly.

I entered through a rose-covered iron gate, climbed the steps to the back porch, sat down at a kitchen table, ate quite a few hot biscuits and jelly, and then proceeded on to school. I do not remember saying anything to the woman.

On the following morning I again turned in at the iron gate, knocked on the back door, and when it was opened seated myself at the kitchen table and awaited developments. The woman must have been surprised to see me, but I was again provided with hot biscuits and jelly. I did the same thing every morning for a long time, and every morning she was ready with hot biscuits and jelly. As I say, I do not remember ever speaking to the woman.

An overall opposite can create and sustain a feeling of

amusement which supports and makes stronger the individual opposites and exaggerations within a piece. In writing "The Albatross" I first decided on an overall opposite consisting of an exaggeration of the wealth and position of the characters contrasted with the rather feather-brained things they say and do. This is the same kind of opposite provided by the valuable statuette, the countess who was dropped from a mountainside, the profile of the Mona Lisa, the Guarnerius violin, and the governor in the bottom of a bucket. One pushes two things in opposite directions in order to obtain as much contrast as possible. In "Test" the opposites are mostly plain to see. In "The Albatross" many of the opposites are not particularly discernible.

THE ALBATROSS*

"Would fingerprints remain on a drinking glass after having been immersed in the sea for three weeks?" I asked.

"Whorls and that sort of thing, you mean?" said Woxley.

"Quite."

"Fingerprints?"

"Exactly."

"Fingerprints, eh?"

"Yes."

There was a long pause while Woxley screwed up his eyes reflectively. "No idea," he said at last. "Why do you ask?"

"No reason," I said.

Actually, the reason I had asked was that in attempting to get myself a drink of water while aboard Deering's ninety-two-foot yacht, Flaunt, I had accidentally opened the sea cocks and the vessel had gone to the bottom within three minutes. Woxley had sent his man out in a pinnace and picked us up, and Deering had already bought a new yacht, so that was all right.

84

The Hidden Opposite

The trouble was that Deering wanted me to put him up for the yacht club. It was a bit awkward. We are just a trifle circumspect. Picky, if you will. In a sense, I owed Deering a favor, especially if they brought his yacht up and found the glass with my fingerprints on it.

On the other hand, Deering is slightly underbred, and his family fortune is founded on the manufacture of tea-bag strings. As it turned out, I needn't have worried. I had forgotten that a mere three blackballs forever bars one from membership.

As is our custom, Deering had been given the run of the ground-floor clubrooms while his application was being considered, and one evening we were sitting around the fire, brandy convenient at our elbows, when Wollinscroft said, "Has it ever been vouchsafed to you to see ball lightning?"

"The sort with branches?" said Woxley.

"No," said Wollinscroft. "No branches. Ball-shaped."

"Absolutely not," said Woxley.

"In the summer of 1963," said Wollinscroft, "it was vouchsafed to me to see ball lightning at my summer place in the Berkshires. Two windows, and two windows only, were open at the time—one in the morning room, and one in the library. Well, sir—"

"Did it go in one window and out the other?" asked Deering.

"Yes," said Wollinscroft slowly. "Yes, it did."

"Did it circle the room first?"

"Yes."

The next time I saw Deering was at our annual Procession of Lights. On a cool, fair evening, eighteen yachts, beautifully lighted alow and aloft, chugged slowly past the club float.

85

"They have the same thing in Venice, during the season," said Deering from his seat next to me on the clubhouse porch. "Except that the yachts are luch bigger. Hundreds and hundreds of large yachts, brilliantly lighted, file past the palaces on the Grand Canal. Then the fireworks. Then the theatricals."

Beaufort joined us, with the news that the Hargraves mansion had burned to the ground. "The family was saved," said Beaufort, "thanks to the bravery and intelligence of their dog, Satchville-Belvoir. Apparently, Hargraves was awakened in the middle of the night by the faithful animal tugging at his bedclothes. Then the noble and sagacious creature barked loudly to arouse the other members of the household, and led them all to safety."

"A similar thing happened to a friend of mine," said Deering. "*Their* dog, Prince, not only awakened the family and led them to safety but the noble and sagacious animal then dashed back into the house, only to reappear a few moments later carrying in his jaws the family's insurance papers, wrapped in a damp towel."

"Is that so?" said Beaufort.

A day or so later, Deering appeared for his final interview with Willoughby, the chairman of our membership committee. Willoughby handed him the form that all prospective new members must fill out, and Deering had already written his answer to the first question ("Are there any Democrats and/or Lindsays in your direct line of ancestry? If none, write 'none' ") and was studying the second when Willoughby asked him the name of his new boat.

"Sea Spray," said Deering.

"Indeed?" said Willoughby. "By an odd coincidence, it was on a yacht named Sea Spray that I experienced the most thrilling adventure of my life. It is a story of reckless courage, involving a golden-haired three-year-old girl and a monster shark. Would you care to hear the story?"

"Yes, indeed," said Deering.

"It was off Barnegat Light," said Willoughby. "The child had tripped over a davit and fallen overboard. In a trice, she disappeared from view. Well, sir, I dived in—"

"And saved the child?" said Deering.

"Well, yes," said Willoughby.

"Did you encounter the shark?"

"Yes, I did."

"But you fought it off?" said Deering.

"Yes."

"Amazing," said Deering. "Is that my membership card?"

"No," said Willoughby. "You will be notified in the usual way."

Curiously, Deering's membership card never came. He waited around for several months, and then sailed his boat down the coast and joined a yacht club with six cement gnomes on its front lawn.

"The Albatross" begins with an exaggeration of the common difficulty of comprehending a question which has nothing to do with what went before. In addition, failure to comprehend a perfectly clear question is an opposite.

Woxley's question, "Whorls, and that sort of thing?" is an opposite because except for whorls there is nothing else similar to whorls to be found on a fingerprint, and the repetition of the word "fingerprints" is an exaggeration. Woxley's inquiring as to whether whorls and that sort of thing is "meant" is an opposite because there is no possibility of anything else being meant.

The emphasis on Woxley's thinking, by screwing up his

eyes and remaining silent for some time is an exaggeration of the process of thinking. Since such profound concentration is supposed to result in some useful conclusion, Woxley's finally saying, "No idea," is an opposite.

Normally there is some reason for a question, so that to say there is "no reason" for a question is an opposite, and the fact that the answer is a lie is another opposite.

The likelihood of the police checking sunken drinking glasses for fingerprints is so remote and Woxley's fear that they might be found so baseless that they are both exaggerations.

To pretend that a sea cock is an ordinary faucet is an opposite. Attempting to get a drink by opening a sea cock is an exaggeration.

The fact that Deering has bought another yacht is an opposite because it does not make everything "all right," except in the sense that Deering has so much money that the cost of a yacht is insignificant, which is an exaggeration.

Owing Deering a favor because he has sunk his yacht is an understatement and all understatements are exaggerations.

The term "slightly underbred" suggests a standard so high that almost nobody could meet it and is another exaggeration.

The word "vouchsafed" in connection with ball lightning is an exaggeration, since it gives an incident more importance than it has, and its use by Wollinscroft is an opposite because it suggests that he is a very humble person, which he is not.

The fact that Wollinscroft, the teller of the story, is not allowed to tell the story is an opposite, and so is the fact that the story was obviously going to be fairly long and turns out to be fairly short, and was going to include a lot of details and no details are forthcoming. Convincingness is achieved through the reader's recognition of the technique of Deering's interruption and familiarity with the fact that people are always finishing other people's stories for them, the reader himself having often begun a story by saying some such thing as, "The fellows at the club bet me I couldn't break ninety," only to have his wife reply, "And you broke ninety?" To which there is no answer except "Well, yes."

The interruption itself is an opposite, since one is not supposed to do that, and the basic opposite is strengthened by the manner in which the story is begun, which seems to preclude any interruption.

The Procession of Lights is presented as something good, so Deering's comment suggesting that it is no good becomes an opposite.

Beaufort's story of the dog is an exaggeration because what the dog actually did (bark) is a small thing in contrast to the emphasis on the dog's bravery and intelligence, and the fact that one might really expect more from a dog named Satchville-Belvoir.

Deering's story, besides being an exaggeration of the usual heroic dog stories, carries the same kind of opposite as his tactless description of the yachts of Venice.

Deering's interview with the chairman of the membership committee has the exaggeration of the conceit of Willoughby in assigning himself "reckless courage," and contains an opposite in his enormous desire to tell the story, which comes to nothing.

There are various other opposites strewn through the piece (the more the better) such as the fact that one reason a millionaire with a perfectly good yacht is denied membership in the club is because of tea-bag strings. And there is an implicit basic statement of a group standard of behavior which is exaggerated throughout, down to the final distinction between people who think cement gnomes are fine and those who don't.

The next example is a piece by Bill Nye, written in 1887,

which demonstrates that Bill Nye knew all about the function and use of opposites in 1887. He abandons the bad spelling of his contemporaries and simply has fun, partly, I suspect, because he is writing it for a local newspaper and doubts if he will get paid.

I have just returned from a private rehearsal of a new operetta of which I am the author, and hasten to write a fair, honest criticism of it for the press. In this criticism I shall try to be perfectly frank to mention any defects, and yet I shall try to avoid hurting the author's feelings. I want to score the operetta with a merciless hand, and yet I do not wish to give myself needless pain.

The operetta itself is called "The Singed Cat," because it is really so much better than it seems to be. The music was composed partly by myself and partly by a count who plays on the ferryboats in summer and has his winters to himself. He does not wish to have his name used, because, as he says, he is afraid that "foreign powers will get on to it and make him come back to attend to the count business again." He says it is very disagreeable to be a count and live on a long, slim pedigree and what the neighbors bring in from time to time.

The orchestra opens the performance with a selection from the "Flying Dutchman." Difficult as it may appear, the orchestra makes a good selection from this gentleman, and it is played well after everything is ready. It takes some little time for an orchestra to get ready, however. The man who bites off the first joint of the clarionet breathes a few liquid notes, the first violin sounds "A" and the gentleman with the bassoon looks up into its dark recesses to see if any cayenne or kittens have been deposited there since he played last. The superintendent of the large violin stands it up on end and feels of its staccato. He then chalks his bow and the leader whispers in a low voice to the man who salivates the cornet. The snare drum soloist gets his assortment of drums into a semi circle, hangs his triangle where he can get at it, runs his eye over the xylophone, sleigh bells, bird call, picket fence, bones, castanet, cymbals, Swiss bells and fortissimo. The leader writes his autograph in the atmosphere with his stick and the band goes into committee of the whole with a wild snort. A difficult piece then follows. Some of the audience are heard to state that they wish it had been so difficult that the orchestra could not have played it.

The curtain now rises, and a primary school of over 800 pupils is seen passing in review across the stage, singing a song of forty-nine verses, meantime going through a system of calisthenics. In making one night stands with "The Singed Cat," most any primary school will do with a few rehearsals for this chorus. Get these children secured in advance and all their parents will come to see how the children look on the stage. I thought of this myself.

A beautiful soprano now comes on, accompanied by her voice, and wonders where Felix is. She decides to sing a small song while waiting for him. The song is an arpeggio with diatonic scales on it. It begins low and fluttering, like the cry of a wounded clay pigeon, and gradually soars upward, like the price of coal, and ends with some artistic gargling which suggests a warble in the upper register.

As she gets more confidence in herself she becomes more irritated because Felix did not get there at the same time he said he would.

The prima donna of the "Singed Cat" has a pleasant

voice, full of timbre and fine allegro movement, border-
ing on the andante. Mr. Riley, who has heard her, says
that when she pulls out the last joint on her crescendo
and opens her upper register, her mouth looks not unlike
a stab in the dark. She sings with the whole arm movement, and her action is good as she goes by the judges'
stand. She has a selection in the second act called "Back
to Our Mountains," in which she starts off with a retard
in which she emits a chest note which tests the acoustics of
the hall, that she is tickled to get back to her mountains,
such as they are, and is pleased with the altitude. She has
assisted in "The Damnation of Faust," but otherwise her
conduct has been good. She is a widow, her husband being deceased. He was listening to the song of a buzz saw
near Stillwater, Minn., in 1875, and got an idea that the
saw had something confidential to communicate and desired to take him apart for that purpose. Anyway, he was
in that condition when they found him. For that reason
her music was frequently tearful and often solfeggio in
spots. Her repertoire is very large and has a lid on it. The
only criticism that I feel warranted in making, and I hate
to do that, is that she has slightly ruptured her voice by
trying several years ago to sing a duet with herself and
thus draw two salaries.

When the applause has died away Felix comes in with
a baritone voice and diminished triad. He thinks of the
first voice while the piccolo makes a few desultory remarks, and then he explains how he could not get there
when he agreed to, because the jury disagreed, or something of that kind. He swallows an imaginary clam with
the shell on it, and begins in a low, passe roundelay
which develops into a duodecimo run. He is accom-

panied by a running mate, consisting of a flute with a large red mustache over the main entrance.

"The Singed Cat" will be produced at the Polo grounds early in January. Let there be a full house.

He begins immediately with an opposite, for no reader will believe that he is going to write a "fair and honest" criticism of his own opera. This is followed by a second opposite in his saying that he will be perfectly frank to mention defects and at the same time try to avoid hurting the author's feelings, he will be merciless, yet he does not wish to give himself needless pain.

The first sentence of the second paragraph is a double opposite, the reason given for naming the opera being pure nonsense and an opposite with lovely convincingness, the second opposite consisting of the reader's already aroused suspicions that the opera is not going to be "better than it seems to be."

The count who helped compose the music lives on a "pedigree," and this is not the last time Nye will manipulate a pun by taking advantage of the fact that in 1887 a majority of his audience were not entirely sure of the meanings of certain words, including "pedigree." The second half of his opposite, the count living on "what the neighbors bring in from time to time," besides contrasting with the generally exalted notion of a count, gained more immediate recognition in 1887 than it would now.

His insult to Wagner, in the third paragraph, is expertly constructed to result in a delay of 5/6 of a second before the average reader discovers that Nye's basic statement is that Wagner never wrote anything worth listening to.

Nye again depends on his reader not being absolutely certain of the meanings of certain words when he says that while the orchestra is getting ready to play, the bass violin player "feels of its staccato."

When the soprano appears Nye uses three puns in a row: she is "accompanied by her voice," there is a pun on the word "scales," followed by a simile in which the song "gradually soars upward like the price of coal."

Throughout the piece Nye makes punning use of technical musical terms, confident that because of the reader's slight uncertainty as to the precise meanings of the terms, he can fool the reader for the split second necessary.

The best of them, and the most daring, is "Her repertoire is very large and has a lid on it." Here the poor reader, who was pretty sure he knew what "repertoire" meant, is forced to think that it might be a box, or something. This idea he immediately rejects, but not before he has laughed.

It is a perfect example of changing the meaning of a word in midstream, and in its structure parallels exactly Henny Youngman's changing the meaning of the word "take," in "Take my wife. Please," but is a lot better. In this choice of words and form Nye reaches the extreme limit of believability, not merely with a pun—a mentally visual pun—for he has no word in mind that strongly resembles the word "repertoire." Instead he changes the real word "repertoire" into a nonsense word comparable to Lewis Carroll's Jubjub bird.

Not everything written in 1887 was this good.

13

Ridicule

Ridicule is not necessarily funny but it can be made funny if there is some sort of truth at the bottom of it and the exaggeration is apt. Adolescent ridicule is one thing and the profound and deft ridicule of Voltaire or Henry Morgan quite another. It is a matter of expertise. The juvenile accepts the first piece of ridicule that comes to mind and is satisfied with it. The members of a sophomore musical show are quite happy with something Noël Coward would discard over his breakfast coffee.

I owe my present chest expansion to a bit of ridicule I concocted at the age of twelve. Every school day for four years I was chased home from school, a distance of three miles, by a slow-thinking but muscular redhead twice my size, who had every intention of striking me with his fists.

Since I could run twice as fast as he could there was little chance that he would catch me. After a burst of speed I would take advantage of my lead to pause and write on the sidewalk in chalk my derogatory couplet:

Pete, Pete, go wash your feet,
The Board of Health's across the street.

Pete would steam up to my message, stop to read it, and chase me with renewed fury.

Children dread ridicule before it happens and arm themselves against it. They become ten times as sloppy as necessary in order to show they don't care. If they fear the nonarrival of an invitation they say, "I wouldn't go to the party if I was invited."

Adolescent ridicule begins with nose-thumbing, schoolboy hoots, comments such as "So's your old man" and "Ten times anything you say," and proceeds to collegiate derision. The horror of ridicule continues through life—fear of bankruptcy, fear of loss of hair or loss of wallet. The fear of going to an alumni dinner will send some men to the gymnasium and most women to the beauty parlor.

Some people take ridicule better than others. It is a common experience to fall down and to wish to resume one's former position of dignity. How one reacts depends upon how vulnerable one is to criticism. The most prissy would be the most vulnerable and least want to look like a fool, whereas a man with true inner dignity can afford to risk a little of it.

Defense against ridicule takes the form of joining in the general laughter and appearing to be amused, or of hostility consisting of such ripostes as "Oh, yeah?" or "You think you're so hot," or of breaking into sobs. An insecure man cannot afford to have on the wrong necktie and is always quavering for fear he will use the wrong fork. Someone with the assurance of Churchill sees many things as absurd, including himself.

Ridicule calls attention to the fact that there is a tiger

96

present, that there is either an opposite or an exaggeration detectable in the thing ridiculed, that some standard of generally agreed-on values has been violated. The standard violated may be, and frequently is, a personal standard developed by an individual within a group.

It is the same structure that is present in telling a joke. The hearer laughs because he is seeing the tiger for the first time. It is being pointed out to him by the teller of the joke.

Ridicule is aggression but ridicule is not funny by itself and a humor structure must be added to it. Sarcasm is addressed to a person in terms he will understand. When a group of tourists visited Picasso's atelier Picasso was painting at his easel and was somewhat bothered by one housewife. "Don't talk to the driver while the bus is in motion," Picasso told her.

Sarcasm and ridicule are not humor structures, but irony is an intrinsic opposite, since one says one thing and means another. The victim is unlikely to catch the nuance because the villain is busy feigning ignorance. If Basil Rathbone is at the helm as Sherlock Holmes the irony is very biting. Holmes was full of ironies directed at Dr. Watson.

Irony is polite and civilized and does not hurt anybody too dumb to get it. Lestrade got blistered all the time as Sherlock Holmes ironically exploded the false premise the fool was working on. Irony is slipped in as a code for those who understand and goes over the heads of those who do not understand.

One may certainly speak of aggression in connection with humor. But I think that aggression lies in the character and not in the humor structure. Some people are aggressive and some are peaceful. When an aggressive person is threatened his aggressive feelings are summoned up at slight provocation, or none at all.

Wit expresses a thought with humor. The thought is one

thing, the humor structure another. No matter how thoroughly they are stirred together they are two separate things. The thought is not funny. The humor structure is.

Aggression sometimes accompanies a humor structure but it is not a part of it. Invective by itself is not funny. In company with a humor structure it is called satire. Criticism is a judgment. A judgment is not funny, but the humor structure that accompanies a judgment might be funny.

In reviewing a play, Dorothy Parker said, "The House Beautiful is the Play Lousy." When Rousseau published his poem "Ode to Posterity," Voltaire said, "This poem will never reach its destination."

Both of these judgments are accompanied by aggression in the form of sarcasm. Sarcasm alone is notoriously not funny. But both judgments are accompanied by a humor structure which presents the judgment in such a way that there is a point to get. Both gain the valuable split second during which the reader is required to transpose the witticism to its original basic statement: This play, or this poem, is no good.

When wit accompanied by aggression is directed at a person there are two tigers present. One exists in the person ridiculed. Let us say his hair is too long, according to the social code of the wit (who wears a crewcut) and is therefore an exaggeration of the "proper" length of men's hair. This exaggeration constitutes an attack on the wit's idea of correctness. In self-justification he ridicules the long hair, thus defending the correctness of the length of his own hair.

When such long hair for men comes into fashion, and is accepted by the wit's social group as correct, he no longer sees anything to ridicule and must wait for a further exaggeration, such as men wearing hair to the waist, or pony-tails, before he is again attacked and must again defend his position by making another witticism.

Ridicule

The second tiger is the witticism itself. It is a humor structure which attacks the judgment and knowledge of the wit's companions. When they see the point of the witticism they laugh. Individual elaboration of the values of a social group result in an individual sense of humor, enabling one to ridicule a painting which is taken seriously by other members of the group.

What is called "cruel humor," such as ridiculing infirmities, is perhaps based on the fact that the subconscious mind does not recognize any distinction among attacks. If a tiger is present, it seems to him, a tiger is present.

In the days when cruel humor was more common, so was drawing and quartering and beheading, and it was not uncommon to gather at the guillotine to pass the afternoon with a few friends. In recent years the conscious mind has succeeded in taking over, and has decided that infirmities and such shall not be laughed at, and that anything considered to be cruel, or even mean, shall not be tolerated.

Nevertheless, in the presence of certain forms of insanity, or of certain bodily afflictions, which result in forms of behavior far removed from the normal, the poor dumb subconscious mind, knowing no better, presses his electrical button, signalling an attack, only to be instantly and sternly suppressed by the conscious mind.

In jokes such afflictions are usually merely a convention, a cliché that is no more real than the giant in Jack and the Beanstalk. For example, a man was chased by a madman. He ran across a road, climbed a fence, and fled across a field, still pursued by the madman. Out of breath he was caught by the madman, who touched him gently, said, "Tag! You're it!" and ran off as fast as he could in the opposite direction.

In the old days, when everybody carried swords, chopping people into mincemeat was a part of the ordinary give and take of daily life. People used to cut off each other's heads, laugh heartily, and go have a tankard of ale together.

Today if anyone sticks his finger with a pin he runs to put iodine on it. There are no more fist fights, the last one occurring in 1910, and there are no more dog fights either. The dogs, having acquired the temperament of their masters, go out for walks wearing little raincoats if the weather appears threatening.

In such effete times it is natural that the mere mention of blood (sorry) should be distressing. Nobody wants to see any. There is a long list of other things that nobody wants to see, or hear. This includes jokes that suggest that anything is wrong with anything. Since all jokes suggest that something is wrong with something, humor is going through a difficult period. We have agreed not to hurt each other, like the rooster and the horse who agreed not to step on each other's feet.

At base, ethnic humor seeks to correct errors, and by errors I mean any behavior that differs from that of the lordly beholder, or that is deemed to be correct by his social group. The laughter at ethnic humor is based on self-justification. The reasoning goes: "If he is right, I am wrong."

People are offended by ethnic humor for the same reason that one is offended by laughter at one's serious remarks, such laughter asserting that there is a great difference between our conception and reality. We are offended because the desire to look well to our fellows extends to details we are not consciously aware of, and because the laughter suggests that we have broken a social code, while those who laugh at us subconsciously believe that we are attacking them by trying to make them think that an absurdity is good sense.

In the case of dialect humor the subconscious mind reasons: "If his pronunciation is correct, then mine is incorrect. I will

100

force him to speak as I do by making fun of the way he speaks. To make my point clear I will exaggerate his errors."

Until exaggeration is added by the comedian there is no humor. The European misuse of syntax and pronunciation, or an Irish brogue, is merely charming until by exaggeration it is made into an attack.

Exaggeration of dialect alone is on the level of Josh Billings's deliberate misspelling of words and has very little humor. Amos and Andy did not depend on such weak forms as "I'se regusted." The cliché, assigned to all groups of which one is not a member, is the basic statement of all ethnic humor, the thing that can be exaggerated.

The cliché permits the joke to be brief, and to the extent that the cliché is accepted, convincing. One says, "There was this Scotchman . . ." and the hearer at once says to himself, "Ah, yes. Thrifty. Very thrifty." The joke can now proceed: ". . . who was dying. His wife brought a candle to his bedside and sat with him. Presently she left the room, saying: 'If you feel yourself going, pinch out the candle.' "

In the joke about an old Jewish gentleman who was struck by a car, an idiom is taken advantage of. While waiting for the ambulance a woman in the crowd rolls up her coat and puts it under the victim's head.

"Are you comfortable?" she asks.

"I make a living," he shrugs.

The idiom is rejected as not being in the hearer's lexicon and without the idiom the joke doesn't work, but the humor of the joke lies almost completely in the misplaced emphasis.

14

Satire

Satire and ridicule are pretty much the same thing. One is better done than the other. One might argue that satire is more intellectual than thumbing one's nose, that it has more style and refinement, and is comparatively well mannered.

Ridicule is apt to be an explosion of the moment and not well thought out. Satire, having gone through an intellectual process, is once removed from direct cruelty. Writing an essay about a politician forces one to dig into one's resources. The satirist or caricaturist is working with his stuff, his own artistic and intellectual process. There is enjoyment in the technique of making fun of the subject.

The ridiculer feels more immediate anger. The satirist felt it originally, but his anger has been diffused by his creative process. He has his own technique and applies it to the subject. He cannot sit there in a state of red-hot hate and raise ridicule to the level of art.

Any great satirist can, if he chooses, do a straight portrait or a harangue. Swift and Aldous Huxley sometimes left satire and launched into something else. But a satirist cannot be simply angry. If wit is lost he becomes a pamphleteer, or an old lady shaking an umbrella at society.

Shaw was often too angry to be witty. *Pygmalion* is like a dull fairy story and one knows the ending before one gets into one's seat. Dickens's anger was not so visible and one becomes engrossed in the story. George Jean Nathan was rather scathing and had enormous wit, but he was not a satirist, and had he not been an expert in the theater his work would not have held up.

Satire is a shedding of light by a superior intelligence and cannot be employed by the ruck of people. Or, to put it another way, as Alexander Pope did, it is "to all but Heaven-directed hands denied."

Satire requires a nimble mind, the ability to make leaps of the imagination. One must have a profound knowledge of a subject to satirize it, since it must be carried beyond its normal form and be distorted in order to show its various facets. One needs also a keen awareness of the location of the jugular, because satire borders on cruelty and one must be sure of the weakness.

The satirist's job is complete annihilation. Don Rickles is not satirical because in spite of his bite and sting he is emotional rather than intellectual. It is obvious that he is trying to make us like him. William Buckley is a fine satirist who uses ridicule at a high level, attacking hypocrisy, double standards, and the various mores of politicians, pricking their false fronts with wit. Beyond the laughter there is something learned, a further experience which may be compared to the enlightenment of a Beerbohm caricature. The person or the political situation will never again be looked at in the same way.

How far satire is carried depends on how popular the satirist wishes to be. A good satirist is always out on a limb and willing to be hated, or perhaps feared. Alexander Pope, who was so small that he sat on a pile of books for dinner, and so fragile that he was unable to dress and undress himself, fiercely refused a pension offered to him by a government he despised.

The satirist will never be popular as a humorist, but he is unable to help himself. If one is born with a satirical bent, one looks at everything with a satirical eye. One has a turn of mind that runs to satire, just as some men's minds run to chess or bowling. He is the most honest and probing of humorists and has no wish to avoid responsibility.

Unfortunately for him there are few targets today against which he can direct his witty ire. We don't have monumental people any more. Churchill was the last of them, and the rule of thumb is that one's target must be pretty important. Lyndon Johnson was a moderately monumental character with a lot of warts and the satirist could go to work on him. But he was no Disraeli or Richelieu.

There is today a general bland climate of bland people and bland happenings. The artists are colorless, there are no great egos to be punctured, no *grandes dames* in society, no pundits such as Mencken or Nathan, and nobody in the writing field like Balzac.

There is a uniformity of costume. The eccentric is gone, to be replaced by pseudoeccentrics like the Beatles and writers who grow beards but are otherwise faceless, all of whom talk the jargon that is ground out by colleges. An age of great characters and great happenings is required to produce great satire.

Satire, like ridicule, is a way of pointing out something you hadn't noticed. There is a tiger in the bushes and the satirist calls your attention to it. If you are in a state of hate, the satirist kindly points out to you all the things you unconsciously hate.

A lot of people feel exactly the way Archie Bunker feels but would be afraid to express it. However, since the program has social approval one is permitted to laugh, which is a disguised way of enjoying one's prejudices.

Henry Morgan was once a satirist with true maturity and balance, and real wisdom as well as intelligence. There is a fine line between the sorehead and the satirist. In some ways satire is really a kind of whining and complaining, done in an unexpected way, which throws new light on a subject with some wit.

That is what Henry used to do. Oscar Levant was a borderline scold who rose to heights at times, mainly because he saw so much, most of it in himself. Howard Cosell, however ponderous, tends to satire, and keeps a straight face which is one of the requirements.

Peter Ustinov is a profound humorist who is able to get inside the skins of many different types. His imitations are precise, his ear for accent wonderful, and he is an expert on the subject of idiocy. He is awfully cute about pomposity, and points out the weaknesses and blunderbussing of the establishment in the best possible way.

Shaw was such an old capon, with his vegetarian attitude toward life, that it is clear he could never enjoy a good meal. Ustinov enjoys food so much that when he says something is mildewed around the edges, one pays attention.

Ustinov's satire is structured and planned. Robert Morley is willing to be sillier, takes more chances, and has more fun doing it. Morley does not know as much as Ustinov, improvises more, and goes off on more daring slants. Ustinov has the insights, Morley the wild free sense of fun. Morley disarms one into thinking he is going to say something stupid, but doesn't. On the other hand, Malcolm Muggeridge gives his keen glance and you know something intelligent is coming.

Truth is the main thing. If it is not true it is not satire. In plain humor one can luck something. One can try an opposite to see whether or not it works. Not so with satire. Satire requires an intellectual overview. It is surgical rather than pill-taking, which is why most people fear it and are uncomfortable in its presence. They reason that if the satirist sees this awful thing in *A*, and sees that awful thing in *B*, they don't want to be around when the satirist decides to turn his flashlight on them.

The essential trick of satire is the dextrous stripping away of a facade. If one has his eye on tender feelings he is not a satirist. If a writer loses his sense of humor and goes into a tirade he is no longer a satirist but a haranguer. Satire is a high form, difficult to achieve, requiring objectivity and the kind of perspective that includes a long view, a side view, and a back view, not likely to be acquired by a hothead.

15

Caricature

The caricaturist looks for a weakness, such as too much strength in one feature. As in satire the idea is to destroy the subject. One looks for the key thing. In making a caricature of Gerald Ford, finding the key thing will take a few moments. It does not at once make itself known. He is a good-looking man to begin with, harder than most to do, a difficult subject for the same reason that Eisenhower was a difficult subject.

The caricaturist hesitates for some time before applying his pencil to the paper. He sees all these American features without any eccentricity, and eccentricity is the key thing the caricaturist is looking for. Ford offers only a certain smallness and narrowness of the eyes, horizontal level slits that look at one in a level honest way, like a football coach. There is a rather high bald forehead, a rather small nose, and a football player's jaw.

The fact is, Ford is not a fit subject for caricature except that he is in the public eye. Still, if the caricaturist wants any money he will have to make a drawing, so he goes to work on the high forehead, making it higher, narrows the eyes, makes the nose smaller, and adds an extremely long upper lip.

The caricaturist does his best work with his best subject. One cannot destroy Ford because Ford cannot be destroyed. There are no hidden depths of duplicity, or vanity, or neuroticism. One is much better off with Hubert Humphrey where one can have some real fun with vanity, pomposity, and a political animal with all his equipment.

If the satirist is presented with a soap opera he does not do his best work, whereas a play by Robert Bolt gets his juices flowing and makes him think. But what can he do about *Our Town*? The play itself prevents him from having an opinion. The word "nice" keeps coming into his head. This defeats his purpose as a satirist. It is not a fair target for his greatest darts. But let John Gielgud get on there and it becomes quite a different matter. The lion has strength and can take it, and will survive. At any rate it is fairer than pecking away at a mouse.

The same problem confronts the caricaturist. He has to use whatever is in the face. A poor caricaturist, presented with very characterful features to begin with, is away ahead of the game. Churchill spent a lifetime making himself into a caricature and presented himself full blown to the caricaturist as a gift. This is not to say that a great caricaturist could not dig deeper and come up with more. But a poor caricaturist's superficial rendition of Churchill would have some character in it.

Presented with the fairly remarkable juxtaposition of features in Henry Kissinger, the caricaturist can hardly lose. He has got a nose there that dominates the face, he has got eyes behind which there are all kinds of veiled and hidden thoughts, and it is clear that he is never going to say anything that one can get anything on. One has the chin to work with, which is huge, glasses are always good, and one has the rather thick lips in a kind of twisted smile.

But this is a face that one can find on any cab driver. It is the character that makes it come alive, and the irony and the complication. He presents an unfathomable mix of neuroticism, humor, and intelligence. There are so many sides to his character that he presents a most interesting problem. The main feature of his face is the hiddenness, the veil he has over his face. His face is a conundrum and a puzzle, and unless the caricaturist can decode at least one of the factors he is left with just the physical character, which is itself very interesting.

Like great satire, great caricature must be lethal. If caricature is half baked and consists of pulled punches it is neither a great work of art nor great caricature. It is like knowing karate and not using it. If the best satire and caricature were not lethal there would be no fear of it. If Daumier is put in jail it means someone is afraid of him. If Voltaire is exiled every time he shows up, it means the same thing.

Max Beerbohm punctured egos and was all the more effective for being gentle, a reflection of his own gentle personality. But he was always careful to impale his victims. His caricatures of Swinburne and Dickens transcend reality, just as great caricatures are supposed to do. When one returns to the living person one has been enlightened and feels that the person caricatured has been explained. "So this is what that set of features means, eh?" one exclaims. "I always thought there was something very weak in that face!"

Holbein's portrait of Henry VIII is not commonly thought of as caricature, yet it makes perfectly clear the conniving, deceitful, and hedonistic character of the thrower-of-chicken-bones-around. The portrait has done more to establish the consensus of opinion as to the character of Henry than anything else, and no actor has approached the role who has not studied the portrait.

The person caricatured must be recognized. One must have a likeness. But if it is only that and is without the wit of extreme exaggeration it is not very amusing. The observer says, "Ah, yes. So and so. But why aren't you in portraiture?"

In spite of his dependency on Victorian technique, David Levine is about the best satirist around today. But if he lost his wit the result would be simply big ugly drawings of politicians. Edward Gorey is a good satirist besides being a borderline caricaturist who like Levine has absorbed a whole age in his style of drawing. But his work goes far beyond aping the Victorian manner, and makes fascinating comments on present day life. On the other hand, if one looks at drawings of the period showing people in the same costumes and settings one is bored stiff.

Caricature is quite apart from all other arts in its purpose and is highly specialized. The purpose of caricature is not simply to show the subject, which is the job of the portraitist, but to show the truth, beyond the known truth that the camera would show.

The intentions of the caricatured person must be serious. Gilbert and Sullivan had a lot of buffoonery and burlesque going on about captains and judges, but they are at one end of the spectrum of satire, the other end being occupied by Swift.

Great caricature is lethal, but not all caricature is, and there are degrees of satire. One does what is required. But good caricature always informs life. If one caricatures someone like Caruso one gets one's fun from his ebullience. There is no harm in such a man to begin with and the caricaturist sees love of life, hedonism, and the Falstaffian character.

Some caricaturists withhold the final thrust, but it is more fun to be lethal, and for this one needs the features of somebody like Maugham or de Gaulle. It is not that one can't do Ford, but that one is not interested. He is so nice and the niceness is reflected in his features.

The great prototypes of vanity or evil are easier to do, and at the same time harder to do, because there is so much more there. If there is evil in the face, and the caricaturist really does his work, never again can his fans or his relatives say, "Such a wonderful person!" If a great caricaturist really exposes the evil qualities of Napoleon, it makes no difference how fast he turns out marble busts of himself.

16

Style

Primitive American humor suffered from a lack of literary background. There were plenty of humorous perceptions but little deftness or elegance.

"We have not yet had time," said Josh Billings, "to boil down our American humor and get the wit out of it."

The fact that the United States was such a huge land mass with so much freedom resulted in mistakes that could not have happened in a civilized country. But the "bohunk" humor of those early days joins easily with rural humor everywhere and may be seen in the paintings of Breughel, in which people are dunking buckets of water on each other, behinds are showing, and all kinds of revelry and bauderies are going on.

Early American furniture and something as lovely as quilting hold up because they are art forms. But early American humor does not hold up as an art form. Misspelling in English can hardly have universality, to say the least. The log cabin had charm but does not enter into the realm of architecture.

It was a time of some vulgarity, some coarseness, the humor of the big lie, and the pretended simplicity of Yankee humor. Mr. Dooley represented the Irish immigrant, larding his jokes with such phrases as, "Faith, and it's meself phwat," "Divil a wan, sor," and "Och, shure now, and bejabbers."

Style involves an artistic arrangement of words. It is not a part of one's technique but arises from it, and depends as much on the words one has decided never to use as on the words one has accepted into one's vocabulary. The reader should receive some more or less clear impression of the character of the writer from his style, and in his writing one can see Robert Morley as clearly as in one of those television commercials, flapping around in his tweeds over the English countryside, like a Dickens character, popping up from behind hedgerows with his jolly cross-eyed look, or bicycling through the village graveyard.

These excerpts are from his *Punch* columns on the subject of food:

> I have two distinct approaches when eating out. Quiet confidence, as host—a hint of formality in my manner of greeting the staff. I try to impart a sense of occasion to the ritual of seating my guest and choosing the food and wine, adding a touch of originality by asking for the salt to be taken away until we have need of it. "I don't know if you feel as I do," I remark to my friend, "but I cannot bear a cruet with the aperitif." The use of the word *cruet*, here, is, I flatter myself, not without courage. Occasionally, before ordering the meal, I will summon a waiter and enquire about his wife. "Better, I hope?" I tell him. I don't actually know whether the fellow has a wife but he will not care to correct me, though he may look a little puzzled—but I am confident that my companion

will mistake his bewilderment for gratitude. The impression I wish to give—and, I have no doubt, succeed in giving—is that of the late Noël Coward in charge of a happy ship: the crew's troubles are my troubles—up to a point, of course. Before choosing the wine, I always say quite simply and, indeed, truthfully, that I know nothing whatever about it. When the others have suitably expressed their disbelief, I suggest we take the wine-waiter's advice. "Something you want to get rid of," I tell him encouragingly. "Perhaps a Sancerre 1958, or Sauvigny de Clos Montard '49?" I usually give a little chuckle as he departs. When he returns with the bottle I am careful not to taste it—this is a privilege I reserve for my guest.

In Kent when I was young there were Sunday teas under a cedar tree and cake stands carried in procession across the lawn and silver trays, and large cups for the gentlemen and small for the ladies. They were not my teacups or my footmen, but for the rest of the week selling vacuum cleaners from doorstep to doorstep I would hug the memory of gracious living and Dundee cake.

Since the war, things have never been quite the same. Two who never came back from the holocaust were Fuller's Walnut Cake and Sainsbury's Breakfast Sausage. I count myself fortunate that in my formative years, and indeed for some time afterwards, I ate my share of both. But tea shops are not what they were, particularly down South, though there is one opposite Kew Gardens which specialises in Maids-of-Honor, and Fortnums still does its duty nobly. Indeed their restaurant off Jermyn Street with its soda fountain is open unexpectedly late in the evenings in case you've missed out earlier, and there is deep consolation to be found in one of their elegant rarebits washed down with a chocolate milkshake.

Do my readers remember, as I do, Gunter's in Berkeley Square and Stewart's in Piccadilly, and the Trocadero in Shaftesbury Avenue? One is tempted to ask what on earth people do in the afternoon these days. Of course there is always the Ritz.

In an endeavor to find out what happened to the trade I looked up tea shops in the *Yellow Pages*, to find the sole listing of such establishments is now confined to Capone, A., 38 Churton Street, S. W. 1. I rang up to enquire about reserving a table, but something in my voice alerted the member of the staff who answered.

"You won't like it much here," he told me, "this is a tea room for working men and we don't reserve." A similar enquiry to Gunter's, now in Bryanston Street, provided a more puzzling response. Tea was apparently available as long as I knew Mr. Vincent, who was out at the moment. I said I looked forward to meeting him and would it be all right if I brought a friend? The voice raised no objection and asked for the name and initial and when I'd given it, the time.

"I thought about four," I said.

"And you're a friend of Mr. Vincent's?" again the fatal enquiry.

"Not yet, but I hope to be a great friend after tea."

"If you're not a friend already, I don't think you'd better come. Who are you, exactly?"

"A member of the public," I replied with unaccustomed humility.

"We've given up entertaining them," the voice rebuked, and hung up.

It must be pleasant to live in Penarth, or, for that matter, at Sully, the next village, where we had a memorable lunch party at Sully House, rightly awarded three spoons in my Michelin, and where you eat in what was once presumably the cellar among rheoboams of old Burgundy. Although I don't normally divulge exactly what I munch on these junkets, I would like to praise the boiled chicken and rice in a cream sauce and once more the asparagus. I feel it is important to eat as much of it as you can, otherwise it might disappear like sea-kale. I don't mind about sea-kale any more than I mind about endives, but asparagus matters to me. I hope it always will. Once a year it arrives on the menus like a visitor from abroad. I suppose you can always get it from abroad at any time of the year but, like strawberries, unless it is domestic it just won't do.

After the feast some of the younger members of the company embarked on a mild streak into the icy waters and across the causeway to an island 500 yards off shore. I watched them till they were up to their knees and then drove back to Cardiff past the notices warning visitors against such folly. I didn't wish to be there when they drowned. What one dreads almost more than anything at my age is being sharply spoken to by a Coroner.

Morley's writing is in a tradition that goes straight back to Shakespeare and includes Oscar Wilde. Wilde has his own amused viewpoint on life, which is a perspective on the importance and nonimportance of things. In *The Importance of Being Earnest* Wilde demonstrates a deft and elegant use of opposites and exaggeration:

LADY BRACKNELL: Are your parents living?

116

JACK: I have lost both my parents.

LADY BRACKNELL: Both? . . . That seems like carelessness. Who was your father? He was evidently a man of some wealth. Was he born in what the Radical papers call the purple of commerce, or did he rise from the ranks of the aristocracy?

JACK: I am afraid I really don't know. The fact is, Lady Bracknell, I said I had lost my parents. It would be nearer the truth to say that my parents seem to have lost me . . . I don't actually know who I am by birth. I was . . . well, I was found.

LADY BRACKNELL: Found!

JACK: The late Mr. Thomas Cardew, an old gentleman of a very charitable and kindly disposition, found me, and gave me the name of Worthing, because he happened to have a first-class ticket for Worthing in his pocket at the time. Worthing is a place in Sussex. It is a seaside resort.

LADY BRACKNELL: Where did the charitable gentleman who had a first-class ticket for this seaside find you?

JACK: (Gravely) In a hand-bag.

LADY BRACKNELL: In a hand-bag?

JACK: (Very seriously) Yes, Lady Bracknell. I was in a hand-bag—a somewhat large, black leather hand-bag with handles to it—an ordinary hand-bag in fact.

LADY BRACKNELL: In what locality did this Mr. James, or Thomas, Cardew come across this ordinary hand-bag?

JACK: In the cloak-room at Victoria Station. It was given to him in mistake for his own.

LADY BRACKNELL: The cloak-room at Victoria Station?

JACK: Yes. The Brighton line.

LADY BRACKNELL: The line is immaterial. Mr. Worthing, I confess I feel somewhat bewildered by what you have just told me. To be born, or at any rate bred, in a hand-bag, whether it had handles or not, seems to me to display a contempt for the ordinary decencie   amily life that remind one of the worst excesses   French Revolution.

Beerbohm avoided profundity as if it were a disease. He created a tiny, microscopic world into which he drew the reader. Almost against one's will one became interested in these totally unimportant people and things. He had a way of changing the world around him to the way it should be—Beerbohmsville.

He would inflate a small crotchet of his own into a *cause célèbre* which one enjoyed because it relieved the tension of one's own crotchet which, up until then, one had not been aware of. It was quite an achievement.

His humility was a kind of conceit in reverse. No matter what subject he attacked, no matter how obsequious an attitude he assumed, he slyly and amusingly injected into the discussion his own quiet qualities so that he was seen at the end to be in the choice position.

There have been many more deadly writers than he but none with his charm and compassion. He had more wisdom than insight and was enormously civilized. His was a small, perfectly honed talent which always served him.

The following paragraph is from his "Porro Unum":

'. . . Who,' you ask, 'would there be to receive the King in the name of the Swiss nation?' I promptly answer, 'The President of the Swiss Republic.' You did not expect that. You had quite forgotten, if indeed you had ever heard, that there was any such person. For the life of you you could not tell me his name. Well, his name is not very widely known even in Switzerland. A friend of mine, who was there lately, tells me that he asked one Swiss after another what was the name of the President, and that they all sought refuge in polite astonishment at such ignorance, and, when pressed for the name, could only screw up their eyes, snap their fingers, and solemnly declare that they had it on the tips of their tongues. This is just as it should be. In an ideal republic there should be no one whose name might not at any moment slip the memory of his fellows. . . . And yet, stronger than all my sense of what is right and proper is the desire in me that the President of the Swiss Republic should, just for once, be dragged forth, blinking, from his burrow in Berne (Berne is the capital of Switzerland), into the glare of European publicity, and be driven in a landau to the railway station, there to await the King of England and kiss him on either cheek when he dismounts from the train, while the massed orchestras of all the principal hotels play our national anthem—and also a Swiss national anthem, hastily composed for the occasion.

Perelman shares with the reader all of the banana peels of life. He deals with the human condition. One partakes of a little adventure in which everything is going to come out wrong. When he satirizes the Victorian style one has the feeling of being told a fairy tale, or of hearing a Dickens story. The form is not infrequently that of a tiny movie, with a heroine and a villain, in which the author casts himself as a bon vivant, a Don Juan, or a cultivated man of affairs who always comes a cropper.

Everything that comes right in such a movie comes wrong in Perelman. At the end he is still throwing good money after bad. He is often on the verge of making a killing but one never sees him speeding to the bank. He is the supreme psychologist, and very good at milking the daydream and the wish. Each piece of writing is a true slice of life no matter how he exaggerates it, and he never gets the better of any of these tailors:

EINE KLEINE MOTHMUSIK*
WAR ON MOTHS BEGINS

The moths are beginning to eat. Even if the weather seems cool, this is their season for gluttony. Miss Rose Finkel, manager of Keystone Cleaners at 313 West Fifty-seventh Street, urges that these precautions be taken:

All winter clothes should be dry-cleaned, even if no stains are apparent. Moths feast on soiled clothes, and if a garment has been worn several times in the last few months, it should be cleaned.

Clean clothes may be kept in the closet in a plastic bag. It is safer, however, to send all woolens to a dry cleaner to put in cold storage.

Customers should check to make sure that their clothes are really sent to a cold storage and not hung in the back of the store.—*The Times.*

Gay Head,
Martha's Vineyard, Mass.,
July 14

Mr. Stanley Merlin,
Busy Bee Cleaners,
161 Macdougal Street,
New York City
Dear Mr. Merlin:

I heard on the radio this morning before I went for my swim that the heat in New York is catastrophic, but you wouldn't guess it up here. There is a dandy breeze

*From *The Rising Gorge,* copyright © 1942, 1952, 1954, 1955, 1957, 1961 by S. J. Perelman. Reprinted by permission of Simon & Schuster, Inc.

at all times, and the salt-water bathing, as you can imagine, is superlative. Miles of glorious white beach, marvellous breakers, rainbow-colored cliffs—in short, paradise. One feels so rested, so completely purified, that it seems profane to mention anything as sordid as dry cleaning. Still, that's not exactly your problem, is it? I have one that is.

Do you, by chance, remember a tan gabardine suit I sent in to be pressed three or four years ago? It's a very expensive garment, made of that changeable, shimmering material they call solari cloth. The reverse side is a reddish color, like cayenne pepper; during the British occupation of India, as you doubtless know, it was widely used for officers' dress uniforms. Anyway, I'm a trifle concerned lest moths get into the closet where I left it in our apartment. The suit isn't really stained, mind you; there's just a faint smudge of lychee syrup on the right sleeve, about the size of your pinkie, that I got in a Chinese restaurant last winter. (I identify it only to help you expunge it without too much friction. I mean, it's a pretty costly garment, and the nap could be damaged if some boob started rubbing it with pumice or whatever.)

Will you, hence, arrange to have your delivery boy pick up the suit at my flat any time next Thursday morning after nine-fifteen? He'll have to show before ten-twenty, since the maid leaves on the dot and would certainly split a gusset if she had to sit around a hot apartment waiting for a delivery boy. (You know how they are, Mr. Merlin.) Tell the boy to be sure and take the right suit; it's hanging next to one made of covert cloth with diagonal flap pockets, and as the Venetian blinds are drawn, he could easily make a mistake in the dark.

121

Flotilla, the maid, is new, so I think I'd better explain which closet to look in. It's in the hall, on his right when he stands facing the bedroom windows. If he stands facing the other way, naturally it's on his left. The main thing, tell him, is not to get rattled and look in the closet *opposite*, because there may be a gabardine suit in there, without pockets, but that isn't the one I have reference to.

Should Flotilla have gone, the visiting super will admit your boy to the flat if he arrives before eleven; otherwise, he is to press our landlord's bell (Coopersmith), in the next building, and ask them for the key. They can't very well give it to him, as they're in Amalfi, but they have a Yugoslav woman dusting for them, a highly intelligent person, to whom he can explain the situation. This woman speaks English.

After the suit is dry-cleaned—which, I repeat, is not essential if you'll only brush the stain with a little moist flannel—make certain that it goes into cold storage at once. I read a piece in the newspaper recently that upset me. It quoted a prominent lady in your profession, a Miss Rose Finkel, to the effect that some dry cleaners have been known to hang such orders in the back of their store. You and I have had such a long, cordial relationship, Mr. Merlin, that I realize you'd never do anything so unethical, but I just thought I'd underscore it.

Incidentally, and since I know what the temperature in your shop must be these days, let me pass on a couple of hot-weather tips. Eat lots of curries—the spicier the better—and try to take at least a three-hour siesta in the middle of the day. I learned this trick in India, where Old Sol can be a cruel taskmaster indeed. That's also the place, you'll recall, where solari cloth used to get a big play in officers' dress uniforms. Wears like iron, if you don't abuse it. With every good wish,

Yours sincerely,

S. J. PERELMAN

New York City,
July 22

Dear Mr. Pearlman:

I got your letter of instructions spelling everything out, and was happy to hear what a glorious vacation you are enjoying in that paradise. I only hope you will be careful to not run any fishhooks in your hand, or step in the undertow, or sunburn your body so badly you lay in the hospital. These troubles I personally don't have. I am a poor man with a wife and family to support, not like some people with stocks and bonds that they can sit in a resort all summer and look down their nose at the rest of humanity. Also my pressing machine was out of commission two days and we are short-handed. Except for this, everything is peaches and cream.

I sent the boy over like you told me on Thursday. There was no sign of the maid, but for your information he found a note under the door saying she has quit. She says you need a bulldozer, not a servant, and the pay is so small she can do better on relief. Your landlady, by the way, is back from Amalfi, because some of the tenants, she didn't name names, are slow with the rent. She let the boy in the apartment, and while he was finding your red suit she checked over the icebox and the stove, which she claims are very greasy. (I am not criticizing your housekeeping, only reporting what she said.) She also examined the mail in the bureau drawers to see if the post office was forwarding your bills, urgent telegrams, etc.

I don't believe in telling a man his own business. Mine is dry cleaning, yours I don't know what, but you're deceiving yourself about this Indian outfit you gave us. It was one big stain from top to bottom. Maybe you leaned up against the stove or the icebox? (Just kidding.) The plant used every kind of solvent they had on it—benzine, naphtha, turpentine, even lighter fluid—and knocked out the spots, all right, but I warn you beforehand, there are a few brownish rings. The lining was shot to begin with, so that will be no surprise to you; according to the label, you had the suit since 1944. If you want us to replace same, I can supply a first-class, all-satin quarter lining for $91.50, workmanship included. Finally, buttons. Some of my beatnik customers wear the jacket open and don't need them. For a conservative man like yourself, I would advise spending another eight dollars.

As regards your worry about hiding cold-storage articles in the back of my store, I am not now nor have I ever been a chiseller, and I defy you to prove different. Every season like clockwork, I get one crackpot who expects me to be Santa Claus and haul his clothing up to the North Pole or someplace. My motto is live and let live, which it certainly is not this Rose Finkel's to go around destroying people's confidence in their dry cleaner. Who is she, anyway? I had one of these experts working for me already, in 1951, that nearly put me in the hands of the receivers. She told a good customer of ours, an artist who brought in some hand-painted ties to be rainproofed, to save his money and throw them in the Harlem River. To a client that showed her a dinner dress with a smear on the waist, she recommends the woman should go buy a bib. I am surprised that you, a high-school graduate, a man that pretends to be intelligent, would listen to such poison. But in this business you meet all kinds. Regards to the Mrs.

Yours truly,

S. MERLIN

Gay Head, Mass.,
July 25

Dear Mr. Merlin:

While I'm altogether sympathetic to your plight and fully aware that your shop's an inferno at the moment— I myself am wearing an imported cashmere sweater as I write—I must say you misinterpreted my letter. My only motive in relaying Miss Stricture's finkels (excuse me, the strictures of Miss Finkel) on the subject of proper cold storage was concern for a favorite garment. I was not accusing you of duplicity, and I refuse to share the opinion, widespread among persons who deal with them frequently, that most dry cleaners are crooks. It is understandably somewhat off-putting to hear that my suit arrived at your establishment in ruinous condition, and, to be devastatingly candid, I wonder whether your boy may not have collided with a soup kitchen in transit. But each of us must answer to his own conscience, Merlin, and I am ready, if less than overjoyed, to regard yours as immaculate.

Answering your question about Miss Finkel's identity, I have never laid eyes on her, needless to say, though reason dictates that if a distinguished newspaper like the

Times publishes her counsel, she must be an authority. Furthermore, if the practice of withholding clothes from cold storage were uncommon, why would she have broached the subject at all? No, my friend, it is both useless and ungenerous of you to attempt to undermine Miss Finkel. From the way you lashed out at her, I deduce that she touched you on the raw, in a most vulnerable area of our relationship, and that brings me to the core of this communication.

Nowhere in your letter is there any direct assertion that you *did* send my valuable solari suit to storage, or, correlatively, that you are *not* hiding it in the back of the store. I treasure my peace of mind too much to sit up here gnawed by anxiety. I must therefore demand from you a categorical statement by return airmail special delivery. Is this garment in your possession or not? Unless a definite answer is forthcoming within forty-eight hours, I shall be forced to take action.

Yours truly,

S. J. PERELMAN

New York City,
July 27

Dear Mr. Perleman:

If all you can do with yourself in a summer place is hang indoors and write me love letters about Rose Finkel, I must say I have pity on you. Rose Finkel, Rose Finkel—why don't you marry this woman that you are so crazy about her. Then she could clean your suits at home and stick them in the icebox—after she cleans that, too. What do you want from me? Sometimes I think I am walking around in a dream.

Style

Look, I will do anything you say. Should I parcel-post the suit to you so you can examine it under a microscope for holes? Should I board up my store, give the help a week free vacation in the mountains, and bring it to you personally in my Cadillac? I tell you once, twice, a million times—it went to cold storage. I didn't send it myself; I gave orders to my assistant, which she has been in my employ eleven years. From her I have no secrets, and you neither. She told me about some of the mail she found in your pants.

It is quite warm here today, but we are keeping busy and don't notice. My tailor collapsed last night with heat prostration, so I am handling alterations, pressing, ticketing, and hiding customers' property in the back of the store. Also looking up psychiatrists in the Yellow Pages.

Yours truly,

S. MERLIN

Gay Head, Mass.,

July 29

Dear Mr. Merlin:

My gravest doubts are at last confirmed: You are unable to say unequivocally, without tergiversating, that you *saw* my suit put into cold storage. Knowing full well that the apparel was irreplaceable, now that the British Raj has been supplanted—knowing that it was the keystone of my entire wardrobe, the *sine qua non* of sartorial taste—you deliberately entrusted it to your creature, a cat's-paw who you admit rifles my pockets as a matter of routine. Your airy disavowal of your responsibility, therefore, leaves me with but one alternative. By this same post, I am delegating a close friend of mine, Irving

127

Wiesel, to visit your place of business and ferret out the truth. You can lay your cards on the table with Wiesel or not, as you see fit. When he finishes with you, you will have neither cards nor table.

It would be plainly superfluous, at this crucial stage in our association, to hark back to such petty and characteristic vandalism as your penchant for jabbing pins into my rainwear, pressing buttons halfway through lapels, and the like. If I pass over these details now, however, do not yield to exultation. I shall expatiate at length in the proper surroundings; viz., in court. Wishing you every success in your next vocation,

Yours truly,
S. J. PERELMAN

New York City,
August 5

Dear Mr. Perlman:

I hope you received by now from my radiologist the two X-rays; he printed your name with white ink on the ulcer so you should be satisfied that you, and you alone, murdered me. I wanted him to print also "Here lies an honest man that he slaved for years like a dog, schlepped through rain and snow to put bread in his children's mouths, and see what gratitude a customer gave him," but he said there wasn't room. Are you satisfied now, you Cossack you? Even my *radiologist* is on your side.

You didn't need to tell me in advance that Wiesel was a friend of yours; it was stamped all over him the minute he walked in the store. Walked? He was staggering from the highballs you and your bohemian cronies bathe in. No how-do-you-do, explanations, nothing. Ran like a hooligan to the back and turned the whole stock upside down, pulled everything off the racks. I wouldn't mind he wrecked a filing system it cost me hundreds of dollars to install. Before I could grab the man, he makes a beeline for the dressing room. So put yourself for a second in someone else's shoes. A young, refined matron from Boston, first time in the Village, is waiting for her dress to be spot-cleaned, quietly loafing through *Harper's Bazaar*. Suddenly a roughneck, for all she knows a plainclothesman, a junkie, tears aside the curtain. Your delegate Wiesel.

I am not going to soil myself by calling you names, you are a sick man and besides on vacation, so will make you a proposition. You owe me for cleaning the suit, the destruction you caused in my racks, medical advice, and general aggravation. I owe you for the suit, which you might as well know is kaput. The cold-storage people called me this morning. It seems like all the brownish rings in the material fell out and they will not assume responsibility for a sieve. This evens up everything between us, and I trust that on your return I will have the privilege of serving you and family as in years past. All work guaranteed, invisible weaving our specialty. Please remember me to your lovely wife.

Sincerely yours,
STANLEY MERLIN

17

Cartoons

All professional cartoonists first got into the business in order to avoid work. All of them were born with an ability to draw fairly well, and found out that if they would take five minutes to draw two figures facing each other, one with the mouth open, they could take the rest of the day off. There is no such thing as a professional cartoonist who doesn't play golf.

Many cartoonists show an interest in humor at a very early age. Mischa Richter says, "I started drawing when I was two and haven't been able to stop since."

Ton Smits was born in Holland, and it was not long before he was busy. "I wanted very much to become something or somebody funny since as long as I can remember," he says. "Among my early childhood memories I remember clearly that my sisters taught me to walk. One of them sitting on the ground would let me loose and the other would catch me after a few steps.

"When four years old I would ring bells or knock on the doors of neighborhood people to tell self-made humorous stories the moment the door was opened. At the same time I made drawings. I could not yet write, but I drew. Not like other children, but humorous drawings. They were done on white cards which I got from a tailor, cards on which had been pasted samples of cloth. I used ink that I got from a shoemaker, who used it to make leather bluish-black. I can still remember the bad smell.

"Having come of age (twelve), I wanted very much to be a circus clown. In those days clowns were funny—Grock, and the Fratellini. But if one attends college in a middle-big Dutch town with eighty painters, one does not become a circus clown."

Whitney Darrow, Jr., says: "I guess things have always seemed funny to me. With many childish anxieties I think I used humor to counter them and to laugh them away. My father was funny, a thing I admired and tried to imitate. I gravitated to school acting and humorous writing, and in college wrote for the daily paper and ran a humor column. But I never drew a line until I was nineteen, and then it was to illustrate ideas I wanted to submit to the humor magazine. As art editor I had a chance to try all kinds of drawing, and liked doing it so much that after school I just kept on."

At one time most college magazines were humor magazines and, like Darrow, people like Peter Arno and Robert Benchley began their careers by contributing to them. But for the past decade or so there has been an ominous quiet on campus. College magazines dropped humor and began to concentrate on politics. Collegians showed no sense of humor about themselves or about the world. They had been taught not to laugh.

But humor is so life-giving and important that it cannot be suppressed forever. Was streaking the first slight sign of a renaissance? An idiotic thing like streaking is so light-hearted and enjoyable that it suggests a desire to return to innocence,

"They *said* sevenish Tuesday, didn't they?"

Whitney Darrow, Jr.

or to have some just plain simple-minded fun. It was like a breath of fresh air.

The cartoonist begins by thinking of a subject familiar to the public and reduces a part of that subject to a statement of fact or a cliché. He reduces the statement of fact to a particular situation and introduces the opposite of the statement of fact. He spends the rest of his time trying to make it convincing.

A cartoon is not an illustration. One draws a lamp, a chair, or a sofa, and exclaims, "My! What a beautiful sofa!" Unfortunately nobody laughs at a beautiful sofa. It is easy to become confused because one is often dealing with the same subject matter. But the cartoonist and the illustrator have different goals.

In approaching a stock situation in, say, a posh men's club, the goal of the illustrator is embellishment, elaboration, richness, and all the detail he can pour into it. But his best job would be a total defeat for the purposes of a cartoonist. The cartoonist would want to eliminate every last thing in the clubroom, retaining only the irreducible minimum. As soon as the cartoonist has established that it is a club, he is through. The end product is not just different but precisely the opposite.

The cartoonist draws a sofa to let the reader know that the scene is a living room. The illustrator uses a beautiful sofa because he is drawing a tender love scene that will cause the reader to choke up. If an editor chokes up while looking at a cartoon it is merely another rejection. One must keep the eye on the central idea. As Ton Smits says: "If I can make my idea about the people clearer with an ugly drawing, I will not make a beautiful one. Why should a humorous drawing be pretty to look at? Does a clown have to have a nice voice, or a classic profile?"

The illustrator uses tone to allow light to reveal an object. The cartoonist uses tone to keep a character from floating off the floor, or to create convincingness, or to pull a bad pen-and-ink drawing together.

The illustrator, the painter, the sculptor, the playwright, the composer, and the cartoonist all have the same idea—to get a reaction from the reader. The reaction the cartoonist wants is laughter.

Someone once described a cartoon as an idea with a line around it. Michael ffolkes, after saying that Paul Klee once described his drawing process as "going for a walk with a line," adds that he spent six years in formal study of art at eminent establishments and "I can't say whether the experience was a help or a hindrance, but it is extraordinarily difficult to decide how much 'good drawing' is necessary to be a good cartoonist. . . . Unless you are a Thurber it is probably best to learn a little of how to draw."

Mischa Richter had a lot of formal training in drawing and painting, "as well as in the history of art. I studied at the Museum School in Boston, and at the School of Fine Arts at Yale. I don't believe it hindered me at all. On the contrary, it gave me confidence."

Ton Smits spent five years at an art academy and "learned there nothing at all. Nothing I could use, that is. I never really accepted anything, so I had nothing to unlearn."

Apparently if one cannot draw very well in the academic sense it is not as bad as one might think, and if one has graduated with honors from art school it is not as bad as one might think, either. One has to learn to draw a sofa well enough so that it does not distract the reader from what is being said, or one must train oneself to draw a less beautiful sofa for the same reason.

The problem is to get all four legs of a table the same length and get rid of the queer lopsided shape one has drawn and which attracts the reader's eye so that he can't really pay much attention to the idea being presented. One cannot continually

ffolkes

136

"I'd like you to meet Daddy."

137   *Michael ffolkes*

distract the reader's eye by drawing one arm longer than the other or one foot bigger than the other.

This difficulty with academic drawing harasses the cartoonist for varying lengths of time. It is a secret sorrow he nurses. He presents a brave face to the world but he is aware that he cannot draw a kangaroo. Eventually he discovers that it is his own idea of a kangaroo that is important, and not an academic drawing.

Every cartoonist goes through this period of self doubt. At first he can't get all four legs of a table the same length, and can't sell anything. Then he can get all four legs the same length and begins to sell cartoons. Then he can get everything the same length and sells lots of cartoons. But the doubt remains.

Only a few ever really find out that it is not the job of a cartoonist to show the reader what a kangaroo looks like. It is important only to let the reader know that it is a kangaroo. If the reader is anxious to know what a kangaroo looks like he can look in *National Geographic* magazine.

Materials

One of the first problems the cartoonist runs into is the pen point. It does not travel smoothly over the paper and is apt to catch, spattering ink. If the pressure is heavy enough one is apt to snap off one of the flanges of the nib. If one makes a mistake it is in stark black ink. It can be corrected by making a heavier line in the right place, but too many heavy lines result in a mess not easy to erase.

The difficulty is that one cannot forget the pen point. One watches all the time to see what it is doing. Instead of drawing a nose or an arm the cartoonist draws pen lines, momentarily expecting the worst. Halfway down the nose the pen runs out of ink. When one continues there is a lump on the nose where one connected the pen lines. If one draws too fast one gets out of control. If one draws too slowly the pen line wiggles.

Some cartoonists have solved this difficulty by letting the line wiggle. They draw slowly and all of their lines wiggle and they don't care. They have adapted to the wiggly line and have forgotten about it. They now concentrate on what they are drawing. Not on the drawing itself but on what they have to say.

Frank Modell says: "I have a constant fight with my natural enemies, paper, pens, pencil, and brush. I hate them all. The fight is unending, and I am always abandoning one brush for another because of its refusal to cooperate. I use cheap paper because I have so many false starts I would have to be a Greek shipowner to afford the same quantity of good paper."

Most cartoonists agree. Charles Saxon says: "One reason I use the paper I do is that it is cheap. I like to be able to throw away a lot of preliminary drawings and I don't like to feel committed to any beginning. I don't use tracing-paper, but my cheap paper is semitransparent. When I work through it I can't get exactly the same line so the finish is free.

"I use sixteen-pound Strathmore layout pads for pen-and-ink and for Wolff pencil and wash too. For wash I mount it first with a hot press. The size depends on the complication of the drawing. I like to draw figures with heads about one inch high because it seems to give me the greatest control of expression. I use paper 9 by 12 for one figure, 19 by 24 for lots of figures."

Richter says: "Expensive paper tends to scare and awe me. It's easier to throw away a relatively cheap paper when there is a mistake and start over."

Darrow likes a slight grain: "I use Bainbridge #80 or #170, sandpapered for texture, or Strathmore layout pad paper 14 by 17 inches dry mounted on poster or illustration board.

"I make preliminary sketches from 2 to 12 inches wide and finished drawings usually 10½ by 13. I use a trace light and transfer the sketch to illustration board and then use Wolff pencils, H to 3B, all kinds of charcoal: vine, NuPastel, regular pastel, and compressed charcoal sticks, as well as India ink with pen and brush, and lampblack washes."

ffolkes is happiest working on good-quality watercolor board, using an Iridnoid nib: "I also employ a vast array of pencils, hard and soft crayons, water colors, felt pens, and whatever they think up next.

"All artists, unless they are masochists, eventually find the kind of materials that fight back least. It's a matter of trial and error. My favorite paper is actually a good roughish paper mounted on board. I'm not quite sure why—perhaps it gives a greater illusion of immortality. I tend to work one-half to twice larger than the drawing will appear in print. The reduction in scale tends to knit the composition together and increase the impact."

Ton Smits feels that he has arrived at a simple and direct way to put his drawings on paper: "I cut a piece of typewriter paper into four or six smaller pieces. I sharpen a soft pencil, put its point somewhere on the paper and do my drawing in seconds. I never change anything at all. I just switch on my light table, put pieces of smooth drawing paper over the pencil drawings and go over the lines in black ink.

"Because I like to draw thin lines I keep fifty pens standing in a jar and use each one only for an hour or so. Smooth, high-quality, white drawing paper takes my thin lines most easily."

Most cartoonists spend months searching for a comfortable pen point. One even discovers the music pen, which makes a broad strong line but still wiggles. The carbon pencil seems to be the answer. It makes a black line that will reproduce properly. The catch is that when one makes a mistake it is as difficult to erase as ink.

" Dear Aunt Frieda:
    Thank you very much for the large book..."

Charles Saxon

There are several interesting fountain pens to try. The old Waterman artist's pen is no more, more's the pity, but the Ultra-flex is something like it, and the nonleakable barrel can be filled with India ink. Pelican and Faber-Castell make good fountain pens, and the Osmiroid comes with a variety of interchangable points.

One tries as many pen points as one can find and settles down with one of them, accepting its eccentricities as a part of the technique of pen and ink. In time one is able to treat the pen point with more or less disdain, to more or less forget it, and to concentrate on what one is saying in the drawing.

The Setting

The setting is not drawn for its own sake but simply to further and help make clear the basic idea. The reason for the setting is to let the reader know where the incident is taking place. This will contribute in varying degrees to his understanding of the cartoon. It is of some importance to the reader to know whether the two characters in a cartoon are in a night club or standing in a plowed field.

I asked Saxon how he decides on what environment to use for a specific idea, such as a modern apartment instead of a country house, or walking on a country lane instead of driving a car: "Sometimes there is no choice, of course, but making that decision when the delicacy of furniture taste reflects on the kind of people in the cartoon is fun to do. That is when a cartoon begins to take on an added dimension. Deciding how old the characters should be is challenging too. Sometimes I do the same idea with two different stagings to see how it looks both ways before deciding. The controlling factor is how to make the point most effectively, strongly, clearly, and quickly."

A sofa tells the reader he is in a living room. The setting

will tell the reader what kind of a living room. If the springs of the sofa are broken and the stuffing is coming out of the cushions, the reader will grasp at once that the characters are poor.

Ton Smits does not deal in situation humor if he can help it. "I even hate it," he says, "if I need more for background than a line, or a line and a chair (which informs my reader that something is happening inside a room), or a sun and three flowers (which means in the open air)."

The main idea is to give the reader something he can grasp at once. If one has chosen a sofa as a prop one cannot dawdle over it or draw it in such a fulsome manner that one is in effect entering into a long dull conversation with the reader about how poor the family is, and isn't it a shame they haven't more money? To which the reader will reply, in effect, "Yes, yes. A dreadful shame, but I have my own affairs to get on to."

There is always a single element in a cartoon that the reader will find difficult to accept. This is the opposite one employs and one must attempt to make everything else in the cartoon as convincing as possible.

The reader's subconscious mind runs as follows: This gesture is true, I believe these characters, this is the way people stand and sit, or hang by their heels, the weight of the man's arm would dent the pillow to that extent, and since all of these things are true, so is this thing here.

A little thing will make the reader believe everything. If the attitude of a character, the position of his body, the way he crosses his legs, and the gesture of his arm are all recognized by the subconscious mind as being true, the reader will be momentarily convinced that the opposite in the cartoon is true.

Anything the subconscious mind associates with correctness is convincing. In a Charles Addams cartoon a man is beating off with his umbrella an octopus which has come up out of a

"It doesn't take much to collect a crowd in New York."

Charles Addams

manhole on Fifth Avenue and attacked him. The position of the man and the way he is using his umbrella are both convincing. He is in the correct attitude of a man beating off something.

Rapidly consulting his octopus file, the subconscious mind finds a note to the effect that octopuses live in the ocean. He also discovers that large sewer pipes lead from the city and empty into the ocean. Checking to find out whether the pipes are large enough to accommodate an octopus he finds out that they are.

The fact that some moments later the man's conscious and subconscious mind are having a big argument as to whether in fact the octopus could have got there, in view of the various screens and filters along the route, makes no difference at all, since the reader has already laughed.

The importance of convincingness is not restricted to the setting. The character must be convincing. He must be the character who would be in such a situation, and his gesture must be convincing. What he says must be convincing and he must be the kind of character who would say it.

If the setting is a clothing store it is not enough to show one suit hanging from a rack. If the scene is a family at dinner it is not enough to put on the table one plate, two forks, and a spoon. Nice judgment is required. One must make exact decisions. One must put into one's drawing everything that is needed and nothing that is not needed. If a family of four is having dinner one needs four plates, and there must be food on the table.

The subconscious mind of the reader goes like this: A family of four is having dinner, but there is only one plate. There are only two forks for four people. They are having only meat —no bread, although there is butter on the table. Conclusion: They are having meat and butter for dinner. One man is conveying something to his mouth with a spoon. It must be butter. But nobody eats butter with a spoon, and nobody holds a spoon that way anyhow. Since nobody holds a spoon that way, he is not holding a spoon. Since there is only one plate, four people are not having dinner. Since they are not having dinner, nothing is happening. If nothing is happening there is nothing to laugh at. I will turn the page.

To the degree that a cartoon lacks convincingness it will become less funny. The more convincing the characters and setting the funnier the cartoon becomes. A good idea can be ruined by a lack of convincingness, and a fair idea can be made funny by convincing the reader that the incident is really taking place.

Sketching from Life

The cartoonist rarely uses models. When he seats himself at his drawing board there is nothing in front of him but a blank sheet of paper. With a pencil he sketches in the characters, action, and setting. To be able to do this he will have observed things more carefully than the person who is not an artist.

Frank Modell says: "Sketching from life is important to me, as are the mental notes one makes while observing people. Their faces and bodies express their attitudes and feelings. Their postures and gestures express more than any words they speak, and tell of their history and background, of their likes and dislikes, their hates and loves."

Some artists cannot bring themselves to sketch in public when someone might be watching them. Others carry a pocket sketchbook and are continually making brief sketches of policemen, or of the way people take money from a wallet, or hold spoons, forks, or knives.

Darrow says: "My happiest days are spent with a pocket sketchpad of Strathmore kid-finish drawing paper cut into stacks of 2¾-by-4½-inch sheets, several India-ink pens, and

"Put me down as semi-retired."

Frank Modell

an inconspicuous place on the subway, street or bus, stores, beaches, bars, or parties. For more solid sketching I use a model, a manikin, or a clay figure in a lucite cube."

Some cartoonists are fascinated by the things that happen to the body when people walk. They make innumerable quick sketches, noting such things as where the right hand is when the left foot swings forward, or how much of the bottom of the foot can be seen from behind at the extremity of the action of walking.

Since the only point in making sketches of this kind is to observe and thus to learn, nothing is put down in the sketch except what is observed. No addition is made to the sketch from knowledge already possessed.

Since the parts of the moving figure change their positions and attitudes rapidly, this at first means that by the time one has drawn the line of a forearm it has swung forward and one has no idea of its spatial relationship to the left leg. But continued sketching results in an ability to sum up in one's mind an attitude or gesture and reduce it to a few quick lines.

Ton Smits never sketches from nature "because I use symbols all the time and because it seems to me that symbols express better and more directly what people think. I am not interested in drawing people as they really look. I like to watch people and observe the subtlest things they think, but I never sketch the people."

However, he admits that he is a people-watcher and especially enjoys watching small things: "When I am sitting on the terrace of a sidewalk café I often observe the feet of the people passing by. Everybody seems to walk differently. In many cases the way of walking causes a humorous effect on me. I do not actually laugh at these various ways of walking. It just pleases me to watch. On the other hand, some people walk in a really funny way. You can tell, from walk-watching, whether the people are tired, eager, lazy, poor, young, old, gay, or unhappy, and if they have gone far in life, or are just modest or shy people."

Some cartoonists study the details of rooms, especially doors and windows. They do the same with streets, sidewalks, and storefronts. It is well to understand how such things are put together. A room is basically a box. Once a cartoonist understands the basic structure of an object he can draw as many variations as he pleases.

Research

Saxon has a large architectural file and uses it for reference. "That is," he says, "I use a combination of parts, such as a roof line, a window, or a cornice. There is always the danger of becoming too dependent on references, such as my own sketches, or books, or photographs. I look at the architecture, or the furniture, or the landscape, but I draw freely combining things to make a scene of my own."

When a cartoonist is required to draw a kangaroo or some other object he is unfamiliar with he either goes to look at a kangaroo or reaches behind him, in his kangaroo file, and draws forth a photograph of a kangaroo he had the foresight to clip out of a magazine.

But the clipping should not be allowed to guide the cartoon. The cartoonist may not know anything about kangaroos, but he does know something about animals, and has even developed the basic structure of an animal he likes. The kangaroo is a variation of this basic structure.

What the cartoonist knows about animals and what the animal has to do with the cartoon idea are the important things to get into the cartoon before they are muddied by studying a clipping. The animal's character, gestures, attitude, and expression should all be drawn before turning to the clipping to add such details and make such changes as are needed to make the animal an unquestioned kangaroo.

Richter gave up keeping a research file "because I would forget where I had filed things. I have encyclopedias, a picture dictionary, a Sears-Roebuck catalogue, and various books that I use for reference."

Modell has various research materials, "but my files are always in such a mess that they are all but useless. I use it only when there is something in the drawing I am not sufficiently familiar with, but which I feel must be convincing and authoritative."

ffolkes says he has enormous files on everything, "as I have this awareness in myself of a poor visual memory. But it is a curious fact that after I have spent some time in locating a particular piece of reference, I often give it little more than a cursory glance. Probably it is only there as a psychological reassurance."

This perhaps is the best use of research. While all of the things discussed here have some importance, it should not be forgotten that the single most important thing is to amuse the reader. It is easy to be led off in various directions.

Expressions

There is only one way to get the right expression on a face and that is by feeling it. One must become the character one is drawing and feel as he does. An upturned mouth will tell the reader the character is smiling but will say nothing about his exact state of mind. There are many smiles and one must choose the right one.

Ton Smits says that his own kind of humor almost entirely depends on simplicity "and on the expressions on the faces of the people I draw. These expressions are so important because they make it clear, I hope, what is going on in the minds of the characters I use. All of my better things always deal with what is going on in the minds of people. This is the underlying theme of my work."

Richter says that sometimes the idea depends on the exact facial expression: "The face sets the pace. In most cases one cannot get the exact expression at once and I have often made as many as fifty or a hundred drawings of the face before catching the expression that satisfied me."

The cartoonist must learn to simplify features and to find out what happens to the single dot of the eye, the single line of the eyebrow, and the single line of the mouth, in the forming of expressions.

There are an infinite number of combinations of these three features, when there is taken into consideration the various sizes, shapes, and positions of the dot of the eye and the lines of the mouth and eyebrow. Each of the combinations will produce subtly different expressions with different meanings in different faces and in different situations.

Although the placement and actions of these simplifications of fleshly features are exaggerated, they are still subject to the rules of the movements of flesh and their positions in the face, including perspective. The single line of the eyebrow can be in hundreds of subtly different positions in relation to the dot of the eye. When this number is taken in combination with the possible variations in the size, length, thickness, and direction of the single line of the mouth, it will be seen that a mechanical use of these three elements can result in nothing but a surface expression which means very little.

In simplifying the eye one might take away everything except a dot representing the iris, and a line representing the upper lid. When the eye is rolled up or down the angle of the iris changes, and the dot representing it lengthens as the eye is widened. In the expressions of surprise or fear the eye is

1

2

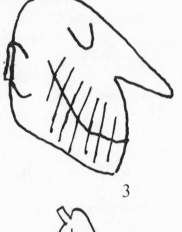

3

4

5

152

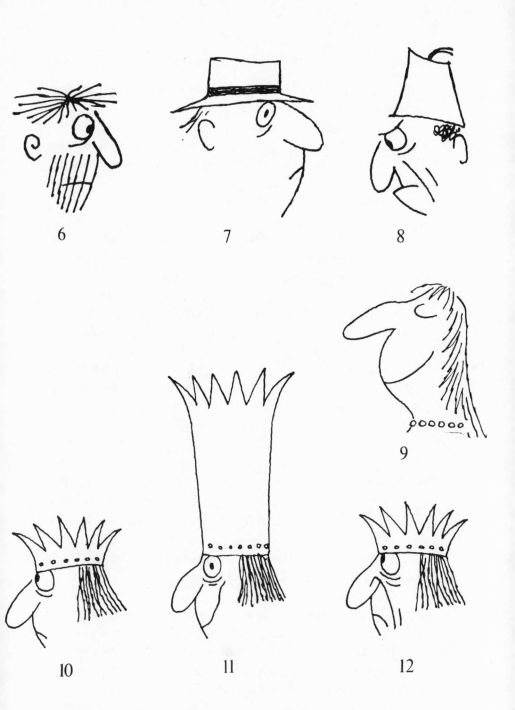

6

7

8

9

10

11

12

Sketches by Ton Smits

wide open and the white of the eye is seen between the iris and the upper lid.

One can exaggerate the widening of the eye to emphasize an emotion, but there is a limit. The limit is convincingness. The reader must be convinced that the eye has widened to the extent shown. Generally, facial expressions are not carried to extremes except to show an exact state of mind, such as extreme fright.

Exaggeration of the features is for the purpose of showing character. Exaggeration of the expression is for the purpose of showing a state of mind. The features and expressions are not exaggerated for their own sake. One does not attempt to make a cartoon funny by drawing a funny face or a funny expression for the same reason that one does not put enormous feet on one of the characters. Big feet or a funny face are merely distractions and militate against the humor one is trying to express in the cartoon. The job is to convey to the reader's mind a humorous idea. The facial expressions will help to make the cartoon funny to the exact degree that they reflect states of mind.

A single vertical lengthened dot of an eye will express the mild surprise of a mind that has not yet grasped what has happened or what has been said. A single short horizontal line of a mouth will enhance this blank expression, which is known as "deadpan." The eyebrow should be level, neither raised nor lowered. The further down from the nose the mouth is placed the more stupid the character will appear to be, although an upper lip too has a limit of convincingness.

Deadpan is a most useful expression. If a cartoonist draws two characters in a proper setting, opens the mouth of the one speaking, and puts a black necktie on him so that the reader's eye will go to him first, the fact is that the character is silent until the reader sees the cartoon and reads the caption.

As he labors through the caption he sees that the second

character has already grasped the whole idea. He can tell from the expression on his face. A moment later the reader sees the point of the cartoon but he doesn't care. In fact he is a little miffed because the second character is brighter than he is, having got the point first. One should always consider the possibility that deadpan is the best expression.

A frown is produced, as you may already have guessed, by lowering the eyebrow. It will be angrier if the eyebrow touches the eye, and angrier still if the vertical crease above the nose is introduced. The mouth is turned down, and turned down further for extreme anger, but if one passes the greatest convincing extreme the mouth becomes less angry. One may wish to add a sneer line from the nose, or one may not. One can find out by feeling as the character feels.

A droopy eye, showing sleepiness or dullness of comprehension can be shown by drawing the upper lid more fully and a quite short dot of an iris touching it. One may show merely the front of the upper lid, or the whole eye may be drawn as an upright oval, in which case a horizontal line drawn through the center of the oval identifies the upper half of the oval as the lowered upper lid.

The eye drawn as an upright oval with the dot of the iris in its center produces a stare. It is least useful when drawn mechanically and most useful when incomplete and more heavily drawn in one part than another as a result of the whole concentration being bent on getting the right expression.

It is then capable of showing extremes of expression not to be had with the simple line of the upper lid and the dot of the iris. It is especially useful in portraying the woebegone, the worriers, and those without hope. In the case of the woebegone the addition of a single line of the bag under the eye will heighten the woebegoneness, as will raising the angle of the eyebrows toward the center and causing them to flatten the tops of the eyes so that they form a piteous, pained look.

156

Sketches by Frank Modell

158

160

Sketches by Whitney Darrow, Jr.

162

Sketches by Whitney Darrow, Jr.

164

165 *Sketches by Mischa Richter*

Certain expressions almost demand the use of the more or less full oval of the eye. It is easier to show that the eyes have been rolled upward in thought, or rolled downward in horror. A greater extreme of the expression of horror can be attained by breaking the oval at the point of the iris and, in the case of a character staring at his grocery bill, an incomplete oval begun just above the iris will best show the character's exact state of mind, especially if the line of the eyebrow is raised to its fullest believable extent so that it accentuates the widening of the eye.

The character speaking should have his mouth open. How wide the mouth is open and its shape will tell the reader a great deal about the loudness of the voice and the manner in which the caption is being spoken.

There is a deadpan speaking mouth in which a horizontal mouth, showing no inclination toward smiling or frowning, is open a moderate width. An open, smiling mouth tells the reader that the character himself knows that what he is saying is amusing, and is a mistake unless that is the intent.

Generally, the wider the mouth is open the louder the voice. If the character is shouting one may wish to open the mouth to the fullest believable extent, and to add the stretch lines that appear in the face, running from the sides of the nose to the corners of the mouth.

The Figure

The cartoon figure simplifies and caricatures the human body in order to establish a character quickly. The cartoonist develops a repertory company ready to spring to life. Each time he draws a cartoon he chooses from this group of actors those who will best express what he has to say.

At the same time there should be an underlying theme so

that one's repertory company consists of the people one knows best and are the proper actors to express one's basic attitudes toward life.

Ton Smits says that the underlying theme in his work is "what goes on in the minds of the characters I use," and that the visualized thinking of these characters preferably deals with human essentials like loneliness: "I think that everybody is at times lonely and entirely on his own and the only solution to this problem is to regain contact with other individuals. This can be done in a sublimized form, in a symbolic way. In my art shop there is only one article for sale—symbols."

One must observe people thoroughly and deeply and draw them again and again, at first exactly as they are. When one understands the basic architecture one studies the nuances and gets to know every blob of fat, the costumes, and where the jewelry settles on them. If one gets the right bosom on a dowager she is a dowager even in a nightdress.

One first strips the figure to its essential form of the big bosom and the double chin. Then one builds it up with choker, high-piled hair, aristocratic nose, and raised eyebrows. One tries combinations of these things and various postures. One must constantly make the vital decisions of what one needs and what one does not need.

If one needs to introduce into the drawing a butler and a Rolls Royce, the drawing is a failure. If the irreducible minimum of the figure says "dowager," one has a cartoon figure. If the cartoonist has an inner understanding of the person he has a character.

Whatever characters the cartoonist chooses for roles in his cartoons must be observed and developed in the same way. The typical expression of the face or the typical posture of the body is the one that shows a character best. Carry either one to an extreme and one's drawing will seem to have the essence of that person.

169

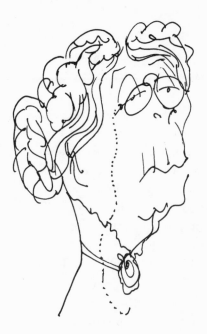

Sketches by Michael ffolkes

171

One should begin to draw the body with the truest gesture of the body, not by diddling about the face, putting in eyes and ears and so on and slowly working down. Instead one should put down an action line which is the whole concept and feeling of the body.

These few quick lines do not look like a body at all, right away. The action line is an attitude, an embryo. When the drawing is finished one should be able to look at the action line and see that the intent was there from the beginning. The action line should contain the truth about the person, a characteristic attitude, perhaps a slump in posture expressing age.

To accomplish this one must try to feel as the character one is drawing feels. One must become an actor, and as far as possible become the person one is drawing. When the drawing is finished one should be able to look at the original action line and say, "Oh, yes. That attitude of the body was there all along."

From the few roughly drawn lines showing the intended shape, the figure is developed by amplifying and filling out the posture. Then one begins to break it down, eliminating complexities and simplifying shapes. If the figure has three chins one encompasses all three in a single line that says three chins. If there are three step-downs to a bulging stomach one draws the whole area in one sweeping line.

One stylizes the figure according to one's own vision. The idea is to eliminate everything one can and get down to an elementary basic shape. One's drawing should still be of a human form. It is not egg shaped, nor is it distorted as Picasso distorted.

One attempts to express a great deal with little, and with style, which can only be arrived at after a great deal of exploration of the true form. The cartoonist's object is to arrive at a simple line that encloses the human form as he sees it. The end is simplification.

Composition

It is necessary to guide the mind of the reader and it is also necessary to guide his eye. In his green, woodland paintings Corot sometimes put a tiny spot of red, a handkerchief on a woman's head, or a workman's shirt, to direct the reader's eye to a center of interest.

Cartoonists achieve the same result with a spot of black, a black necktie, or a black open mouth. A white spot on black will also attract the eye, for the same reason that a single blond in a chorus line of brunettes will.

Perhaps the cartoonist wishes the reader to look first at the person speaking the caption. From that point the lines of the drawing can be arranged to guide the reader's eye to the thing to be seen second. The reader's eye moves along lines easily and crosses lines with difficulty.

If the lines of a cartoon form a rough oval the reader's eye will move around the drawing in a satisfactory manner and be drawn back to the center of interest by the black spot. The eye appreciates rest periods, and white space allows the eye to rest for a fraction of a second before looking at the next thing.

Composition is the form in which one puts the cartoon idea. It is an orderly form. One composes a cartoon in the same way one would set a table. One does not fling the stuff on the table and let the diners figure it out for themselves.

Conventional composition makes use of the order of importance of the objects, and one must decide how much prominence and strength each should have. The more work the cartoonist does the less the reader will have to do.

One puts into the cartoon everything that is needed to make the idea perfectly clear, and puts in nothing that is not needed. If one is serving lobster there will be lobster forks. If not, not. There will be no silver for courses one does not intend to serve.

"Welcome aboard. This is your captain,
Margaret Williamson, speaking."

Mischa Richter

Just as a dinner table is set so that it is pleasant to the eye, so one arranges the space of a cartoon. There should be no confusion. There should be white space. As skilfully as possible one will guide the reader's eye to the telling action.

ffolkes says that the design in his cartoons is largely intuitive and that "the story is everything and most often suggests itself to my imagination in the most direct way it can be told. I never consider more than two ways to arrange a picture, and frequently the composition imposes itself the first time. (Where you place the signature can be an entirely different and much more troublesome problem!) "

Ton Smits says that a good humorous drawing has a different kind of beauty than other drawings, and that "drawing ugly people you can still draw with a satisfying rhythm in your lines, your entire drawing can be in balance. Even so much so that you cannot sign your full name under it and have to use less."

The Finished Drawing

When he makes a finished drawing, says Frank Modell, "I first procrastinate, then jump in, then do it over, and then go back to the original sketch."

"Sometimes," says Richter, "the first sketch works so well that it is the finish."

Sometimes the rough sketch is better than the finished drawing, but can't be printed because some of the parts are so carelessly done that they are distracting. One may have caught an exact expression on the face of one of the characters which reveals clearly what is in the character's mind. Such expressions have a way of disappearing in the finished drawing. So does the balance of effect and the varying degrees of emphasis, done while the idea was crystal clear in the cartoonist's mind.

Darrow says that in the finished drawing "there is the long job of retaining the original spirit of the sketch but at the same time making the idea perfectly clear. I might take many days making dozens of small and large trial sketches, involving a great deal of research, and then do the finished drawing in half an hour."

When a cartoonist makes a rough sketch he is drawing his idea for the first time. As he draws he is forced to concentrate on the character he wants, to feel the gesture he is drawing, and to contort his face into something of the same expression he is drawing. As he approaches the finished drawing all of these things are already done, and the temptation is to think that one need merely trace them off and ink them in.

The trouble is that one always gets on paper what is in one's mind. If one is thinking about being neat, people do not laugh when they see the cartoon. Instead they say, "How neat it is!" The cartoonist must try to recapture the frame of mind he had when he first drew the rough sketch.

The making of a cartoon is a constant procession of choices. One chooses a subject familiar to the public and chooses a particular situation within the subject. One chooses characters which will help make the cartoon idea clear, and chooses gestures and expressions which will help make the characters clear.

A cartoon must be read quickly, and the cartoonist simplifies for the same reason a writer might use one adjective instead of three. The way one chooses to simplify becomes one's style.

Style involves both elimination and design. How much design a cartoonist uses in his work depends on what he wants his work to say. One cartoonist will compel the figure into shapes he likes because he is interested in placing things in a way pleasing to his eye. He is not especially interested in the

4

Ton Smits

characters, which for this reason are less apt to come alive. Another cartoonist is interested in design but never forgets the figure, which is important to him, and will sacrifice anything to get the true character into his cartoon.

All of the cartoonists whose work is represented in this book are fine stylists who have used this process of elimination and choice. They have studied the original realistic form and have eliminated many stages of realism from their drawings.

To give a simple example, Saxon has made the leap from a realistic club chair to his own highly stylized rendition of a club chair. An important part of his work is the fact that he no longer thinks of style. His style has evolved and has become simply his method of saying something.

"The final drawing", says Saxon, "is a kind of spontaneous performance after the play script has been rehearsed, and is not an intellectual exercise. It comes out of my hand. I am not thinking what must be drawn. I know emotionally when it is right and when it is wrong."

The facility Saxon describes is the goal of all young cartoonists, nor is there any reason to despair. It is true that there are many technical considerations in the making of a cartoon, but it is comforting to realize that the cartoonist really has only one problem. The problem is to make the reader laugh.

Index

Index